RULES OF THUMB
FOR BUSINESS WRITERS

Second Edition

Also by Jay Silverman, Elaine Hughes, and Diana Roberts Wienbroer:

Rules of Thumb: A Guide for Writers, 6th ed.
Good Measures: A Practice Book to Accompany Rules of Thumb, 6th ed.
Rules of Thumb for Research
Shortcuts for the Student Writer

By Diana Roberts Wienbroer:

Rules of Thumb for Online Research

By Elaine Hughes:

Writing from the Inner Self

By Elaine Hughes, Jay Silverman, and Diana Roberts Wienbroer:

Finding Answers: A Guide to Conducting and Reporting Research

RULES OF THUMB
FOR BUSINESS WRITERS

Second Edition

DIANA ROBERTS WIENBROER

ELAINE HUGHES

JAY SILVERMAN

McGRAW-HILL

New York   Chicago   San Francisco   Lisbon   London
Madrid   Mexico City   Milan   New Delhi   San Juan   Seoul
Singapore   Sydney   Toronto

*The **McGraw·Hill** Companies*

1 2 3 4 5 6 7 8 9 0   DOC/DOC   0 9 8 7 6 5

ISBN 0-07-145757-7

McGraw-Hill books are available at special quantity discounts to use as premiums and sales promotions, or for use in corporate training programs. For more information, please write to the Director of Special Sales, McGraw-Hill, Professional Publishing, Two Penn Plaza, New York, NY 10121. Or contact your local bookstore.

This book is printed on recycled, acid-free paper containing a minimum of 50% recycled, de-inked fiber.

Library of Congress Cataloging-in-Publication Data

Wienbroer, Diana Roberts.
  Rules of thumb for business writers / Diana Roberts Wienbroer, Elaine Hughes, and Jay Silverman.—2nd ed.
    p. cm.
  Includes bibliographical references and index.
  ISBN 0-07-145757-7 (alk. paper)
1. Business writing. I. Hughes, Elaine. II. Silverman, Jay. III. Title.
  HF5718.3.W54 2005
  651.7'4—dc22   2004030767

CONTENTS

PART THREE: SPECIFIC BUSINESS WRITING

PART FOUR: SPECIAL PROJECTS

PART FIVE: CORRECTNESS—USAGE

PART SIX: CORRECTNESS—PUNCTUATION

APPENDIX

ACKNOWLEDGMENTS

Many friends and colleagues have contributed to this book.

Our late coauthor, Elaine Hughes, provided much of the pizzazz and wisdom in the first edition of *Rules of Thumb for Business Writers*. This revision preserves most of what she wrote, and we trust that she would applaud our additions.

We continue to be grateful for the support we have found at McGraw-Hill. Mary Glenn, Melissa Scuereb, and Jane Palmieri, our editors at McGraw-Hill's Professional Book Group, have been on top of every detail that produced this revision. Lisa Moore, our editor at McGraw-Hill's College Division, has been a special friend to all our books, including this one. North Market Street Graphics created the original design, and MMDesign added a fresh look and some clever enhancements to this revised edition.

Rules of Thumb for Business Writers was written in response to friends in the business world who encouraged us to adapt our college textbook, *Rules of Thumb: A Guide for Writers*, for a larger professional audience. Over the years, their suggestions and questions shaped the concept of this book. In particular, we benefited from the advice of Russell Bosworth, Evelyn Brooks, Joylene Carlson, Leanna B. Fisher, Judy Kelly, and Carolyn Roughsedge.

Special thanks go to Noah Silverman, who gave us the idea and some of the details for the section "Shortcuts for 'Word'"; to Michel Eckersley, for his information on the section "Websites"; and to Emily Hegarty, for advice on key chapters.

A number of colleagues have thoughtfully reviewed *Rules of Thumb for Business Writers*: Anne Gervasi, North Lake College; Gary Christenson, Elgin Community College; Robert Cason, University of Texas at El Paso; Rebecca Fraser, Empire College of the State University of New York; Rebecca Jackson, University of Illinois at

Urbana-Champaign; Caryl Lynn Segal, University of Texas at Arlington; and professional writers Jerry Hill and Gordon Tappar. Our gratitude goes to each of them for careful attention to every aspect of the book.

As always, we want to thank our families—Lance, Noah, and Hannah Silverman, for many suggestions; Carl and Kirtley Wienbroer, for advice on a number of different perspectives.

Finally, we note with great sadness the passing of Jay Silverman's wife, Beverly Jensen. This is the first book in the *Rules of Thumb* series to be written without the benefit of her fine editing eye, her advice on details, and her loving support of the project.

Portions of *Rules of Thumb for Business Writers* have appeared in different forms in *Rules of Thumb: A Guide for Writers*, *Rules of Thumb for Research*, *Rules of Thumb for Online Research* (all from McGraw-Hill), and *Finding Answers: A Guide to Conducting and Reporting Research* (HarperCollins).

A NOTE FROM THE AUTHORS

The phrase "rule of thumb" refers to a handy guideline: The top part of your thumb is roughly an inch long. For some jobs you need a ruler marked in millimeters, but often you can do fine by measuring with just your thumb. Your thumb takes only a second to use, and it's always with you.

We've tried to make *Rules of Thumb for Business Writers* just as easy to use—brief and readable, covering the main writing problems that give trouble to most businesspeople. You can read it out of order, in small doses, to find what you want when you need to solve a specific writing problem, whether in the office, on the job, or at home. In this second edition, we have added guidelines for creating websites, evaluating material on the Internet, using PowerPoint and Microsoft Word, and controlling paper flow.

In this book you will find some points that have to be exactly right, and in those cases we've given the complete details. But where we could, we've given you a rule of thumb—a brief guide that you can use quickly any time you need to compose an effective piece of business writing.

RULES OF THUMB
FOR BUSINESS WRITERS

Second Edition

PART

ONE

THE WRITING PROCESS

1 WRITING IN THE BUSINESS WORLD

Most of the time, you must grab the attention of your reader immediately, or your carefully written material might end up in the recycling bin.

Writing in the business world is not like the writing that succeeds with teachers. In school, you write to demonstrate what you have learned. Teachers usually give you a chance to prove yourself. Remember the math teacher who gave you partial credit for a wrong answer if you had followed the correct procedure? In the business world, however, you can't assume that your audience will be so lenient. You need to put your best effort into every single document you write.

Know what you're talking about. You can't fake it. Everything you write must be grounded in your sure knowledge of what is true.

Take care of errors in punctuation and word usage. Errors in spelling and grammar—even in emails and informal memos—will always work against you.

Follow the basic business forms and protocols. Each professional field follows standard presentation formats. Your office may have a "style sheet"—rules and formats your company has adopted—or there may be sample documents that you can use as guidelines.

Be positive. Most business writing attempts to solve a problem. Always try to be constructive, to praise others where praise is merited, and to offer criticism in terms that are helpful.

▶ IDENTIFY THE KINDS OF WRITING YOU MUST DO

Whether new to the business world or a seasoned veteran, you can benefit from analyzing the kinds of writing required at your office. Examine the current files or seek out a senior colleague who does a lot of writing on the job and who is willing to serve as a mentor.

Categorize the types of documents you regularly must produce both by content and by the types of audience. Take a look at the Table of Contents of this book to see what chapters can best help you become a better writer.

▶ KEEP YOUR READER IN MIND

In many cases, you know who will be reading your memo or report—a specific person or group—and can tailor your style and information accordingly. Knowing your reader allows you to

- Adopt an appropriate style—formal or friendly.
- Stress points your reader will care about.
- Explain points your reader may not know about.
- Address questions and concerns you expect this reader to raise.

Often, however, you do not know the specific person—for example, when writing a letter to a customer. Even when you do know the reader, someone else may see what you write—either now or in the future. For these reasons, it's best to

- Strike a balance between being too informal or too formal.
- Avoid being unnecessarily negative or accusatory of others.
- Make each separate point clear and concise.
- Give credit to the work of others.

Writing is a form of office politics. Be aware of what you put into writing and of who may see it.

2 FINDING YOUR FOCUS

Time spent before you start writing saves time and energy later.

Before you begin any writing project, take a few moments to assess the following characteristics.

▶ THE IMPORTANCE OF THE PROJECT

Who is the intended audience? A report intended for potential customers obviously warrants far more time and psychic energy than a summary of a meeting to be distributed to colleagues.

What is the expected life span of the document? An evaluation that will be part of an employee's personnel file requires more care than a thank-you note. You may want to save a well-written report to present as a justification for your promotion.

▶ THE REQUIREMENTS OF THE PROJECT

What is the purpose? Will you be writing to inform or to persuade? The latter requires more effort.

What is the appropriate tone? Your audience and purpose determine whether you will need to use a formal or informal tone, and whether you will need to spend great care on your phrasing.

How long will it be? Keep in mind that often a short piece of writing requires more effort than a long one. Readers prefer short documents; however, when given an assigned word- or page-count, you should conform. For tips on how to adjust length, see Chapter 9, "Revising."

Is creativity required? In some organizations, originality or style may be primary considerations.

Is collaboration required? If so, you will need to consider the schedules and personalities of the people involved. See Chapter 33, "Collaborative Projects."

How polished does it have to be? Keep your perspective. Don't allow a low-level but urgent project to take time from a more important one with a later deadline.

Remember that your writing reflects on you; errors, even in an email, indicate to some readers that you don't care enough—that you do not bother to get details right.

▶ THE DEADLINE

Allow extra time for drafting, revising, and editing. The length of the product does not determine the production time.

3 SIZING UP YOUR WORK STYLE

To face any writing assignment effectively, you must first face yourself and own up to your actual work style.

Some writers move step-by-step through each phase of a project. They dislike chaos and prefer to work steadily, spreading the work over the full time available. Other writers, however, get excellent results by putting themselves under last-minute pressure. They thrive on tension and excitement. They often work out of order, moving back and forth, writing different parts and reorganizing as they go.

A particular *result* may look the same to an outsider, regardless of the method that produced it. What is important is to identify your own personal quirks and to make the most of your work style.

▶ PROCRASTINATORS AND PERFECTIONISTS: WHAT TO DO ABOUT YOUR WORK STYLE

IF YOU ARE A PROCRASTINATOR

The advantages to procrastination are intensity, concentration, and a sense of adventure. The disadvantages are well known to all procrastinators and their families. A few shortcuts for the chronic procrastinator follow.

Accept that you don't have the luxury of time. Recognize that some aspects of a project may have to be correct but only "good enough," or that some people won't be able to collaborate according to your schedule.

Do at least one thing ahead of time. Pick one step that you don't mind too much and get it out of the way early. Decide on the format, do one freewrite, or read one background article. Pat yourself on the back for having accomplished one part of the job.

Keep a designated place for each project. Make copies of any documents that apply to more than one project, so that each project has a complete set.

IF YOU ARE A PERFECTIONIST

The great advantage of being thorough is that you have time to do a good job. The trick is to stay open, to let creativity bubble up, and to avoid filling time with unnecessary work. Here are some tips:

Don't let panic cloud your judgment. You can reduce a mountainous, overwhelming project to a series of manageable steps.

Don't organize or outline too soon. Allow the creative process to work for you by accepting a time of uncertainty while you gather ideas, talk to colleagues, do some research, and "sleep on it" a while. During this process, keep a notebook handy so that scraps of information and ideas don't get lost.

► Guidelines for Both Procrastinators and Perfectionists

Don't try to make only one draft. You may think you can save time by writing only one draft, but you can't get everything perfect the first time. Actually, it's faster to write something approximately close to the points you want to make, then go back and revise.

Don't get stuck trying to perfect your opening sentence or introductory paragraphs. You can always come back to the introduction once you see how the whole project turns out.

Don't use a dictionary, thesaurus, or grammarcheck before the second draft. Delay your concern for precise word usage and correct mechanics until you have the whole first draft written. Then, go back and make improvements.

Don't write with distractions. When you write, you need to focus your physical and mental energy. You can be distracted by background noise or by being too uncomfortable or too comfortable. You may not even realize how much these distractions can diffuse your energy and concentration.

Know when to quit. Be realistic about the approaching deadline and your own energy level. Allow some additional time for unexpected problems and for fine-tuning your manuscript.

Be smart about files and copies. Until the project is accepted, keep all notes and working documents. Afterward, don't file anything that someone else will keep for you in an easily accessed place. Many documents have already been stored in libraries or elsewhere—in electronic and paper formats, and in several secure locations. Finally, remember that email that you have deleted is still in the company/service provider file.

4 WHAT TO DO WHEN YOU'RE STUCK

For most writers, either *freewriting* (writing nonstop without a plan for ten to twenty minutes) or *brainstorming* (playing with lists of possibilities) will bring good ideas to the surface and show you the way to go.

Sometimes the ideas don't seem to be there, or you have only two ideas, or your thoughts are disconnected and jumbled. Sometimes it's hard to know where to begin or what shape your writing should take. Try several of these techniques, used by professional writers. Some are better for particular writing tasks. For instance, *lists* and *outlines* work when you don't have much time or when you have many points to include. Freewriting works well when your topic is subtle, when you want to write with depth. You'll find several techniques that work for you.

Taking some time before you write will save time later, as the deadline approaches.

▶ DIVIDE THE PROJECT INTO EASY STEPS

Start wherever you're most comfortable. Often, once you have some ideas written, one will lead to another, and you'll soon have a whole draft to work with. Otherwise, try several of the following techniques.

▶ FREEWRITE

Freewriting is the easiest way to begin and leads to surprising and creative results. In this method, you write nonstop for ten to twenty minutes. Ignore grammar, spelling, and organization. Follow your thoughts as they come. Above all, don't stop! If you hit a blank place, write your last word over and over—you'll soon have a new idea.

Then read what you've written and mark the sentences that seem to contain your best thoughts.

Make a list of them and think further about each idea. Sometimes, a freewrite can contain the nucleus of a single important idea. Look for this unifying idea and write it at the top of your freewrite.

▶ Brainstorm: Make Lists, Outlines, or Maps

With this method, before you write any sentences, you make a list of your points, including any examples and details that come to mind. Jot them down briefly, a word or phrase for each item. Keeping these points brief makes them easier to read and rearrange. Include any ideas you think of—reject nothing for now. When you run dry, wait a little until more ideas come.

Now, start grouping the items on the list. Draw lines connecting examples to the points they illustrate. You may prefer to make a "tree" with branches and subtopics growing from the appropriate branch— or interlocking circles or other designs that "map" your ideas.

Then make a new list with the related points grouped together. Decide which idea is most important and cross out unrelated ideas or details. Arrange your points so that each will lead to the next. Be sure to note where examples or facts will be necessary to support your ideas.

▶ Other Techniques to Try

DO SOME RESEARCH

You may be stuck because you need more information. Pick up the phone or email someone who can give you some facts. Spend an hour on the Internet or at your local or office library. Sometimes, just reading related information will give your ideas a jump start.

TALK TO A COLLEAGUE

The idea here is for your colleague to help you discover and organize your ideas—not to tell you his or her ideas. The best person for this technique is not necessarily someone who knows anything about the project, but someone who is a good listener. Ask the person just to listen and not say anything for a few minutes. As you talk, you might jot down points you make. Then ask what came across most vividly. Make notes of what you say in response. Once you have plenty of notes, you're ready to be alone and to freewrite or outline.

WRITE A SHORT DRAFT FIRST

In one page, write your ideas—everything you've considered including. Take just ten or twenty minutes. Now, you have a draft to work with. Expand each point with explanations or examples.

A simple technique is to write just one paragraph—at least six sentences—that tells the main ideas you have in mind. Arrange the sentences in a logical and effective sequence. Then copy each sentence from that core paragraph onto its own page and write a paragraph or two to back up each sentence. Now you have a rough draft. Remember, your first draft doesn't have to be perfect—as long as it's good enough for you to work with.

USE A RECORDER

If you have trouble writing as fast as you think, talk your ideas into a recorder. Play them back several times, stopping to write down the best sentences.

Another method is to write down four or five sentences before you record, each starting with the main word of your topic, each different from the others. As you talk, use these sentences to get going when you run dry and to make sure you discuss different aspects of your topic.

TAKE A BREAK

Even five minutes away from your keyboard can sometimes give your subconscious a chance to work on the project. Some "fallow time" can allow ideas to find you.

USE THIS BOOK

If no coherent plan emerges, take a look at Chapters 2 and 5 ("Finding Your Focus" and "Organizing Your Ideas"). One of the approaches described there may be just right.

5 ORGANIZING YOUR IDEAS

Your goal in organizing is to make sure that your reader gets your major points and that they are arranged in a logical sequence.

Readers in business often want only the point. In most cases, you must provide the rationale or the details, but those should be subordinated to a place where the busy reader can skim them. Headings, bulleted lists, and careful arrangement of your ideas will allow the reader to see the difference between the point and the supporting information.

▶ HIGHLIGHTING YOUR MAIN POINTS

Before you do a final copy and send it to others, be certain that your main point or points stand out. They should be easily grasped, even in a hasty reading.

- Before starting your final draft, write down the major point or points that you want your readers to get. Keep those points in front of you as you revise.

- Arrange a layout so that the main points are easily picked out by the eye. See Chapter 8, "Adding Visual Interest."

- Use a reference line (in memos, letters, and reports) to place your main point right up front and give it special emphasis.

- Repetition of a major point is often necessary in a long document. At times, you may choose to repeat a point to give it added weight. When you do repeat a point, make sure that you use slightly different wording and that you place each repetition in a different context.

▶ CREATING A ROUGH OUTLINE

Some writers need an outline; others write first and then reorganize when they see a pattern in their writing. Still others begin in the middle or write the parts out of order. Some approaches are better for certain topics; some are better for certain audiences. You will need to discover the organization that best enhances the content.

Here's a method that works for many writers:

- Make a random list—written in phrases, not sentences—of all the ideas and facts you want to include. Don't be stingy. Make a long list.
- Decide which are your main points and which points support them.
- Cross off points from your list that do not fit. Remember, you can't put in everything you know without losing focus.
- Decide on your paragraphs—what each will demonstrate and their sequence.
- Now, start writing. Get a rough draft finished before you reconsider your organization.

▶ When to Adjust Your Plan

Your main point may well shift and change as you write. Often, you will come up with better ideas, and as a result, you may change your emphasis. Be prepared to abandon parts or all of your original plan. Some minor points may now become major points.

Here are the signs that you should rethink the organization:

- Some parts are boring.
- Your real point doesn't show up until the end.
- You have repeated the same idea in several places—unless you have clearly done so for emphasis.
- The writing seems choppy and hard to follow.
- Your paragraphs are either too short or too long.

In the end, make sure that you know the main point you want the reader to get and that every sentence contributes to making that point clear.

▶ Using a Formula as a Plan

Ask yourself if you have done a similar project before. If so, you may be able to use the previous document as a model, or you may find other documents in the company files that you can use as a model. See Chapter 31, "Recurring Projects," for some techniques.

Some topics lend themselves to particular arrangements. Lengthy documents might even use different methods of organization in different sections.

COMMON PATTERNS OF ORGANIZATION

A list of points followed by detailed discussion (an introduction stating the main points, followed by a section on each point). This pattern is often used in a business proposal or in a letter of recommendation.

Good news/bad news In the business world, disappointing news often must be communicated. The idea behind this pattern is that you begin with the positive before bringing up the negative. Of course there may be times when you will want to reverse this order.

Problem and solution You state the problem up front and then lay out the solution or solutions that you are recommending. At times, you may have to describe a number of less effective solutions to contrast with the solution you prefer.

Cause and effect As with problem/solution, you state the cause up front (or explain the "situation") and then enumerate the effects that will derive from this cause. (For example, explain a new company policy—the cause—followed by the specific effects this policy will have on employees.) You may reverse this pattern if your purpose is to explain the causes of something—a success or failure, for instance.

Chronology (the sequence in which events occurred). This is often the most logical order for laying out a problem, defending a decision, or persuading a reader to join a particular effort.

Narrative (the story that explains your main point). Telling the story is often used for performance evaluations, letters of recommendation, background, or informal newsletters.

Process (the specific steps for how something has been or should be done). Use this pattern whenever you give instructions or propose a project. Be certain that each step is logically and correctly arranged. See Chapter 23, "Instructions and Directions."

The news lead (the four Ws—*who, what, when, where*—always used in news articles). Sometimes *how* and *why* are included in the opening information. This is a good method to follow for most routine communications, such as announcements, memos, reports, minutes, and so on (who, what, when, where—followed by the details—plus how and why).

Comparison (similarities and differences). This pattern is especially useful when you have two distinct options for which you want to show the pros and cons. Comparison can also be used when you want to highlight or contrast the differences among several options. Depending on what you wish to emphasize, you can discuss each option separately, in its entirety (apples, then oranges). Or you can organize by points of comparison, discussing the options as you go (apple and orange juices, nutritional values of apples and oranges, shelf life of apples and oranges, uses of apples and oranges in cooking, and so forth). Either way can be effective, as long as you are consistent.

Classification (types and categories). This is a useful organization when you have large amounts of information to communicate. Sometimes, information naturally falls into a particular classification; if not, you can always create logical categories as a way to organize material.

Generalization followed by examples or arguments Use this pattern when you want to build evidence in favor of your argument or example. You link your points to a main point; in other words, you move from the general to the specific. You can also reverse this pattern by beginning with specific arguments or examples and then ending with a general statement or idea that these specific examples suggest.

If what you want to say fits one of these patterns, following the pattern can help you organize more quickly.

6 PARAGRAPHING

Use paragraphs to lead the reader step-by-step through your ideas.

Each paragraph should make one point, and every sentence in it should relate to that one point. Usually the paragraph begins by stating the point and then goes on to explain it and make it specific.

Paragraphs should be as long as they need to be to make one point. Sometimes, one or two strong sentences can be enough. At other times, you might need as many as eight or more sentences to explain your point. Paragraphs give readers a visual landing, a place to pause; so use your eye and vary the lengths of your paragraphs. However, the trend in modern business writing is to avoid long paragraphs.

In business letters or reports, block format is the standard form:

- Single-space between the lines.
- Skip a line between the paragraphs.
- Do not indent the first line of paragraphs.

For example, this page uses block format.

FEATURE THE POINTS OF THE PARAGRAPH

When you have a number of points in a single paragraph, you can make them easy to follow.

Enumerate Them

Your handling of this account has been extremely disappointing. First, Ms. Temple reports that you did not reply to email or voice mail messages for days at a time. Second, when you did respond, you were abrupt and didn't allow her time to explain what she needed. Third, when the order you authorized finally arrived, it didn't meet the written specifications.

Break Them Out with Bullets

You have covered yourself with glory in handling Phil Blume's account:

- The time you spent with him during the flood last month made rebuilding possible.
- Your advice saved him time and money in the Johnson City plant.
- Your professionalism and courtesy are the reasons he is granting us the Amarillo project.

BREAK UP LONG PARAGRAPHS

A paragraph that is more than ten sentences usually should be divided. Find a natural point for division, such as:

- A subtopic
- A variation or contradiction
- The start of an example

EXPAND SHORT PARAGRAPHS

Too many short paragraphs can make your thought seem fragmented. If you have a string of paragraphs that consist of one or two sentences, you may need to combine, develop, or omit some of your paragraphs.

Combine

- Join two paragraphs about the same point.
- Include examples in the same paragraph as the point they illustrate.
- Regroup your major ideas and make a new paragraph plan.

Develop

- Give examples or reasons to support your point.
- Cite facts, statistics, or evidence to support your point.
- Relate an incident or event that supports your point.
- Explain any important general terms.

Omit

If you have a short paragraph that cannot be expanded or combined with another, chances are that paragraph should be dropped. Sometimes you have to decide whether you really want to explain a particular point or whether it's not important.

CHECK FOR CONTINUITY

Within a paragraph, make sure that your sentences follow a logical sequence. Each one should build on the previous one and lead to the next. Link your paragraphs together with transitions—taking words or ideas from one paragraph and using them at the beginning of the next one. See the next chapter, "Continuity" for help with transitions.

REMEMBER A BASIC PATTERN

If you have trouble with paragraph organization, you can usually rely on this basic paragraph pattern:

A main point stated in one sentence

An explanation of any general words in your main point

Examples or details that support your point

The reason each example or detail supports your point

A sentence to sum up

Following is a sample paragraph illustrating this basic pattern.

We recommend that this traditional service station be replaced with a high-tech gas station/convenience store. By high-tech, we mean six pumps fitted with credit/ATM/cash machines, the latest pollution controls, and a secure monitor within the store. The volume on this corner will be better served by a facility geared toward sales, not repair service. A similar renovation of our Stewart Avenue station increased sales by 45 percent in the first six months of operation. The transformation could be completed by late fall 2005 if we follow the schedule that worked so well on Stewart Avenue.

7 CONTINUITY: USING TRANSITIONS

Transitions are bridges in your writing that take the reader from one thought to the next.

You need transitions between paragraphs that show the movement from one idea to the next, and you also need transitions to connect sentences within a paragraph.

Often, what seems like a continuity problem (the ideas feel choppy) is actually an organization problem. When your sequence of ideas and points is logical, transitions between the ideas come much more naturally and easily. Therefore, if one point doesn't fit smoothly, you may need to make a list of your points and toy with their order.

▶ USE TRANSITION WORDS

Here are some choices of transition words you can use to illustrate certain points or relationships:

Adding a point:	furthermore, besides, finally, in addition to
Emphasis:	above all, indeed, in fact, in other words, most important
Time:	then, afterward, eventually, next, immediately, meanwhile, previously, already, often, since then, now, later, usually
Space:	next to, across, from, above, below, nearby, inside, beyond, between, surrounding
Cause and effect:	consequently, as a result, therefore, thus
Examples:	for example, for instance
Progression:	first, second, third, furthermore
Contrast:	but, however, in contrast, instead, nevertheless, on the other hand, though, still, unfortunately

Similarity:	like, also, likewise, similarly, as, then too
Concession:	although, yet, of course, after all, granted, while it is true
Conclusions:	therefore, to sum up, in brief, in general, in short, for these reasons, in retrospect, finally, in conclusion

▶ USE REPETITION OF KEY WORDS

• Repeat the word itself or variations of it.

> Everyone agrees that David Stevenson is intelligent. His intelligence, however, does not always endear him to his customers.

• Use pronouns.

> People who have hypoglycemia usually need to be on a special diet. They should, at the very least, avoid eating sugar.

• Use synonyms—different words with the same meaning.

> When you repot plants, be certain to use a high grade of potting soil. Plants need good rich dirt to thrive.

▶ USE TRANSITIONAL SENTENCES TO LINK PARAGRAPHS

Usually the transition between paragraphs comes in the first sentence of the new paragraph.

> Even though Ms. Barbieri followed all these useful suggestions, she still ran into an unforeseen problem.

> Because of these results, the researchers decided to try a second experiment.

Notice that, in these examples, the first half of the sentence refers to a previous paragraph; the second half points to the paragraph that is beginning.

8 ADDING VISUAL INTEREST: LAYOUT, ILLUSTRATIONS, AND POWERPOINT PRESENTATIONS

Layout has become an essential element of all documents.

Computers have made creating your own format and graphics an enjoyable challenge. Add to that possibility all the charts, graphs, drawings, diagrams, and photographs readily available from other sources and you could easily get into the habit of illustrating your point in nearly every document that you write.

Although everyone loves to look at visuals, don't make the mistake of just filling up space with cute or interesting pictures that have nothing to do directly with what you have written. If you just stick in something to create interest, you could well take your reader away from the point you are making.

▶ GUIDELINES FOR LAYOUT

Even if you are not using visuals in your document, you can enhance anything you write by creating a layout that will make your document appealing and easy to read. Keep these simple rules of layout in mind:

- Feature the main points—either in a summary at the beginning or with headings or sidebars.
- Use a consistent and uniform layout throughout.
- Use bulleted lists to break up the text.
- Use boldfacing for major ideas and summary sentences.
- Use subheadings whenever possible, especially in a long document.
- Use data boxes to set off important material.
- Plan ahead for attachments to the document, such as appendixes, forms, and other supporting materials.

Notice that we have used both bulleted lists and boldfacing of major ideas in this chapter, as well as in others. It is fine to use different features as long as you don't haphazardly mix them. Be sure, however, not to overuse any of these features. Bulleted lists and boldface, for example, can become monotonous.

▶ GUIDELINES FOR ADDING VISUALS TO TEXT

When your presentation is primarily in words, visuals should support, not distract.

Make sure each visual has a definite purpose. A visual should either give additional information or clarify information.

Keep it simple. Each visual should communicate a single idea. Enlarge or crop photos if necessary.

Place visuals into the text right at the point they support—or place them all together in an appendix at the end. Place a commentary and explanation of each image right above or below it. If you prefer to put all the illustrations in an appendix at the end, insert a reference for each visual into your text at the appropriate place.

Give the source of the illustration. Get permission before you publish copyrighted images. Beneath the visual, give information on where you found it: title of publication, author, publishing information, and page number. See Chapter 30, "Crediting Outside Sources," for proper documentation.

▶ GUIDELINES FOR PRESENTATIONS— POWERPOINT, WEBSITES, AND BROCHURES

When your presentation is primarily visual, text should support, not distract.

Illustrate the ideas. Use colors, graphs, pie charts, drawings, or photos wherever possible.

Avoid clutter. Make each visual big enough to be easily seen. Sometimes one large picture is much more effective than four tiny ones.

Make sure that the arrangement of your images is logical. If necessary, add headings that explain the sequence (for example, dates for chronological order, sequential positions for exterior to interior, labels for basic to fully equipped). Viewers naturally "read" images from left to right, then from top to bottom. Use arrows, zooms, or captions to draw attention to the features you want the viewer to notice.

Use captions to explain each image. Identify people, locations, or the significance of a particular element.

Clockwise, beginning with Mrs. Astor (in hat) . . .

Bradley Hall in 1953, before the first renovation

Keep commentary brief. Use short sentences or minimal phrases so that the viewer can focus on the image.

For PowerPoint presentations, minimize text and give explanations orally. You don't want your audience to still be reading the screen while you are talking about the next point. Write out only your main talking points. For further suggestions for using visuals with presentations, see Chapter 34, "The Spoken Word."

9 REVISING

Revision is not just fixing errors. It means taking a fresh look at all aspects of your writing, moving some parts of it, and completely rewriting others.

This chapter can serve as a checklist for any document you write, whether short or long. First read your draft aloud; then examine it from the following angles.

YOUR POINTS

- What is the most important point? Make sure it is prominently positioned and emphasized.

- Look for any points that are repeated or unrelated. Make appropriate cuts.

- Make sure your conclusion puts what you've written into perspective.

YOUR AUDIENCE

Even if this is a formal report for a faceless, mass audience, imagine a person actually reading your report.

- The opening line should snag the reader's interest.

- Look for places that sound stiff or artificial. Write the way you would talk to this person.

- Use *you* and *I* or *we*, if appropriate.

TROUBLE SPOTS

Look at the parts that are giving you trouble.

- Do you really need them? Are they in the right place?

- If you got tangled up trying to say something that you consider important, stop and ask yourself, "What is it I'm trying to say, after all?" Then, say it to yourself in plain English and write it down that way.

LENGTH

How to Make Your Document Shorter

Usually, business writing needs to be concise and easy to grasp—as a courtesy to the reader.

- Look for repetition. There is no need to give the same information in more than one place unless you are clearly doing so for emphasis.

- Remember your reader. How much does your specific reader need or want to know? Look for minor information that might bore your reader or distract from the main facts.

- Don't pad your writing. See Chapter 15, "Trimming Wordiness."

How to Make Your Document Longer

Adding words and phrases to a report makes it, at most, an inch longer. Adding new points or new examples will make it grow half a page at a time.

- Build up what's good. Select the good parts, and write more about them.

- Add an example or explain your reasons to clarify your point—or even add a new point.

- Mention other views of the subject that differ from yours. Either incorporate them (showing the evidence for them) or disprove them (telling why others might accept them and why you reject them).

- Add details (facts, events that happened, things you can see or hear). Details are the life of good writing. Instead of writing, "Ms. Aznavour is a real team player," write, "Ms. Aznavour worked on the Collins account with four others. I observed how she filled in during a colleague's absence, met the holiday deadline in spite of a delay in shipping, and did all this with good humor."

- Expand your conclusion. Discuss implications and questions that your report brings to mind.

but

- Don't add empty phrases, because they make writing boring. Make sure that you're adding real content.

CLARITY

- Look for places where your reader might not be able to follow your reasoning.
- Make sure you've demonstrated each point with specific details.
- If you expect a response, be sure you've spelled out both what you want and when you need it.

STYLE

- Check that you've written with energy, using strong verbs, short snappy sentences, and brief paragraphs. See Chapter 14, "Writing with Energy."
- Use transitions (such as *accordingly, therefore, nevertheless*) to show the relationship between ideas. See Chapter 7, "Continuity."
- Write important sentences several ways until you find the best phrasing. See Chapter 16, "Varying Your Sentences."

FORMAT

- How does the final product shape up? It should be easy on the eye.
- Use headings or bullets to emphasize key points.
- Your readers should be able to quickly find out what they want to know.

10 PROOFREADING

The key to proofreading is doing it several times.

Careless errors undermine what you have said, so make a practice of proofreading methodically.

Here are some tips to help you spot mistakes.

MAKE A BREAK BETWEEN WRITING AND PROOFREADING

Always put a little distance between the writing of a document and the proofreading of it. Set the project aside—at least for twenty minutes if you can. That way, you'll see it fresh and catch errors you otherwise might have overlooked. When you write under a deadline, train yourself not to write straight to the final moment; give yourself at least a few minutes to catch your breath. Then proofread your document several times before sending it.

USE YOUR COMPUTER'S CHECKING PROGRAMS

Although they aren't infallible, spellcheckers and grammarchecks can help you locate obvious errors.

Be very conscious of how the automatic correction feature operates: The computer is often oblivious to context and may have changed your mistyped *for* to *of*. It will not alert you to a correctly spelled but inappropriate word—like *accept* versus *except* or *pour* versus *pore*. See Chapters 37 and 38, "Commonly Confused Words" and "One Word or Two?"

SEARCH FOR TROUBLE

Assume that you have made unconscious errors and really look for them. Slow down your reading considerably, and actually look at every word.

PROOFREAD FOR ONE TYPE OF ERROR

If punctuation is your biggest problem or if you always leave off *-ing* endings when you type or if you always write *it's* for *its*, go through the document checking for just that one problem. Then go back and proofread to check for other mistakes. See "Shortcuts for 'Word'" in the appendix of this book on setting up automatic corrections.

PROOFREAD OUT OF ORDER

Try starting with the last sentence and reading backward to the first sentence; or proofread the second half first (usually, that's where most errors occur), take a break, and then proofread the first half.

PROOFREAD ALOUD

Always try to read your document aloud at least once. This will slow you down, and you'll hear the difference between what you meant to write and what you actually wrote.

LOOK UP ANYTHING YOU'RE NOT SURE OF

Use this book and a dictionary.

PROOFREAD ON BOTH COMPUTER SCREEN AND PAGE

First, scroll through and make corrections on the screen. Double-check places where you have inserted or deleted material. Because the eye is more accustomed to noticing errors on paper, you should print and proofread a draft of all important electronic documents before sending them.

PROOFREAD YOUR FINAL HARD COPY SEVERAL TIMES

It does no good to proofread a draft of your document and then forget to proofread the final hard copy. This problem crops up often, especially under pressures of deadline. Remember: A typo is just as much an error as any other error.

11 STAYING ON TOP OF THE PAPER FLOW

Take the time to get on top; then it's much easier to stay on top.

ASSESS ALL INCOMING CORRESPONDENCE

Ask your regular correspondents to use accurate subject lines so you can respond if they have an urgent request. A quick glance can allow you to sort everything into priority order. Distinguish between:

- Documents that need a response

- Documents of temporary importance—for instance, information that you'll need to keep handy for a specific project

- Documents of lasting importance

PLAN YOUR READING TIME

- Read your urgent correspondence and react to it first.

- Defer careful reading of all nonurgent mail until you also have time to react to it.

- Control interruptions by email. Turn off the email notifier while working on projects. Instead, plan to read email at several intervals during the day.

- Read multiple messages from the same correspondent in sequence (sometimes it's more efficient to read them in reverse chronology).

- Designate a specific file for reading material you can defer to "found time"—for example, while traveling, waiting for an appointment, eating alone, and so forth. Decide whether to print any items that are in electronic format.

PLAN YOUR WRITING TIME

When you read your mail, respond to it—and then discard or file each piece of paper or email.

You can draft a quick response to your messages as soon as you read them, but then defer hitting "send" till you have time to revise for tone and accuracy—and to proofread.

Develop a few templates for quick responses—for example, a two-liner

> Thanks for your message. I'll get back to you before the end of the week.

See the appendix of this book for more suggestions.

STORE FILES ELECTRONICALLY WHENEVER POSSIBLE

If your email program doesn't provide an easy way to store your mail in folders, cut and paste important messages into another program.

Sometimes it is more efficient to print out a document and work on the hard copy, then enter the changes electronically.

DON'T KEEP UNNECESSARY COPIES

While you are working on a project, keep all relevant documents and notes handy. (See Chapter 3, "Sizing Up Your Work Style.") You may also choose to use an electronic storage service (a good, short-term solution when working on a huge project). After the project has been accepted, retain only what is necessary for your career. Don't keep anything that someone else will keep for you in an easily accessed place.

ORGANIZE THE PAPER YOU NEED TO KEEP

It helps to have a specific place in your office for all materials (even Post-its) related to each project. Make copies when a document applies to two different projects.

Some print documents should always be kept on file. Make hard copies of electronic documents important to your company or to your career, and consider storing copies in two locations for safety.

See Chapter 2, "Finding Your Focus," for further ideas.

PART
Two

WRITING
WITH POWER

12 STEPS TOWARD A CLEAR STYLE

Readers have little patience for having to search for a point. Be brief, direct, and concrete.

▶ GIVE YOUR READER THE PICTURE

Write for people—real ones. Think of your specific readers and "talk" to them on paper.

Don't delay or bury your point. Instead, be direct and straightforward. Start right off with what you have to say.

Show **the reader what you mean.** Highlight the big fact or create a memorable picture with words.

▶ USE EXPLANATIONS AND EXAMPLES

You know what you mean because your experience lies behind your statement. Add an example or explanation to share that experience with your reader.

> Mr. Llewelleyn trains his sales associates thoroughly. For example, he rotates all areas of departmental responsibility, pairing a newcomer with a seasoned staff member.

> This quarter was marginally successful—by that, I mean that although profits were slightly below those of the last quarter, that loss was offset by the improved efficiency of the billing department.

Sometimes a hypothetical example can support your point.

> What if, when you retire, your pension couldn't cover a catastrophic illness?

▶ MAKE THE POINT EASY TO FIND

- Keep your paragraphs short.
- Use headings and bullets.

- Write short snappy sentences.

- Use simple concrete words.

- Emphasize your main idea in several places throughout.

▶ Above All, Be Specific

Details give life to your ideas. As you write, you naturally concentrate on your ideas, but the reader will best remember a strong example or fact. Therefore, underscore each major idea with strong details.

- A memorable fact

    The corporation's first business venture was not in real estate financing but in developing a biodegradable laundry detergent.

- A statistic

    Less than half a century ago, Wilco employed only 3 people; today, it employs 153,000.

- An anecdote

    Before Mavis Long and Peggy Schultz began their successful bridal consulting business, they were two housewives who had never worked outside their homes. Suddenly, they found themselves with lots of spare time and a major skill they'd developed over the years: planning weddings from start to finish.

- A real-life example

    Trang Lee arrived in this country with little English but incredible musical skills. The enclosed CD demonstrates how appropriate his style is for this project.

- A hypothetical example

    Imagine a state-of-the-art, multimedia presentation that won't decimate your profits.

- An explanation of an abstract or technical term

    By vision, I mean that Carly has both a sharp sense of each client's needs and an accurate view of the purpose of each project.

This simple goal of being clear develops power in your writing.

13 WRITING TO PERSUADE

The art of persuasion stands at the core of nearly all business writing.

Most writing intends to either inform, entertain, or persuade. The best writing combines all three. Although you may think of business writing as primarily imparting information, a close look will usually reveal a subtle request or a streak of soft-sell persuasion.

Even a memo announcing an upcoming meeting will often contain the essential information and then a "push" for attending the meeting:

> This is the Benefits Committee's final meeting of the fiscal year, and we have several very important decisions to make. Please be there!

This is persuasion in its simplest form.

Just being aware of some of the principles of persuasion can add power to everything you write.

▶ CLARIFY THE OUTCOME YOU WANT

Ask yourself what is at stake. What do I want to happen as a result of this communication? Write down the answer as clearly as possible and then keep it before you as you develop your communication. Keeping this single objective in mind will automatically sharpen your writing. For example, your objective may be as simple as one of these:

> I want the company to win this account without having to drop our prices.

> I want the manufacturer to replace the copy machine with a new one and to give us a discount for all the frustration we've been put through.

> I want upper management to provide a day care center within the building. It will eventually pay for itself in improved job attendance.

I want to be promoted to the new position. I meet all the qualifications and feel that I have earned this promotion because of my accomplishments for the corporation over the past three years.

▶ Target Your Audience

In the business world, you rarely write for one person alone; usually, what you write will be circulated among managers, committees, departments, and so forth.

Think about the people you need to persuade and keep these points in mind:

- Most people are naturally loyal to their initial point of view.

- Often, two people can interpret the same facts differently.

- Most businesspeople are extremely busy and impatient with lengthy discussion. They respond best when shown how an idea will benefit them.

▶ Develop a Strategy

Sometimes you can persuade just by asking for what you want and then supplying the rationale, but often you will need to be more subtle. If you are dealing with a reluctant, even hostile audience, you'll need a thoughtful approach. It may be more effective to come at the subject softly or indirectly. For example, you might first want to explain the needs for a given course of action before presenting the recommended action.

However, if you are dealing with a highly charged situation, carefully rethink your strategy. Sometimes a face-to-face meeting might be the best first approach.

▶ Open Appropriately

Gain your reader's attention and goodwill before launching into your arguments. Here are some possibilities.

- Open with a fact.

  > The average business worker has 3,000 email messages on file. (Selling a training session to raise employee consciousness about the legal issues related to email messages)

- Begin with your most persuasive point.

  > We all know that parking problems are a factor in employee tardiness. (For a proposed shuttle bus service)

- Begin with a story or metaphor.

  > Fran Perry is a typical account executive. Her day begins . . . . (For an argument for flextime)

- Begin with a question.

  > Could you use more reading time? (Proposing an audio library for the office)

- Open with a startling comment.

  > I'll bet you didn't know that the average Canada goose defecates every three minutes. (A request for a new policy for the Municipal Parks Department)

- Begin directly with what you are seeking.

  > I am writing this letter to ask you to vote against the proposed change of vendors. Here are the reasons why I am against this change.

▶ STRIKE A POSITIVE TONE

In writing to persuade, it is particularly important that you use an inviting (that is, not alienating) tone. It is possible to argue your point of view without offending others. You can be both polite and strong at the same time.

Use a conversational tone without being too informal or too ingratiating. Strive to sound like yourself—your very best self, your persuasive self. Ask for what you want in a direct, yet harmonious, way.

▶ BUILD YOUR EVIDENCE

In building the evidence to support your request or point of view, you will make a stronger case if you follow these general guidelines:

- Make very clear what you are requesting your readers to do and give strong reasons why they should comply with your requests.

- Emphasize the benefits you expect (who will benefit and how).

- Don't confuse the issue by adding unnecessary details or arguments.

- Use facts and statistics to back up your position.

Give each point a separate paragraph. If you have more than two or three points—or arguments—you may want to consider using a heading above each paragraph so that your main points can be quickly read.

Decide on the order of your points. Sometimes, all the arguments are of equal value; if so, present them first in a bulleted list. Usually, however, there is one you will consider the most important. If so, put your major idea up front, just in case your readers only skim the document.

If you are presenting your evidence in a lengthy document, add a short cover letter in which you clearly but briefly state your position.

▶ END WITH AN OPEN DOOR

You can never assume that you have persuaded your readers. Persuasion often takes place over time, and some communications will require follow-up letters, meetings, or phone calls. However, no matter how carefully you have presented your ideas, there will be times when you will fail to persuade others to your point of view.

Even when the answer is no, you will want to get that answer as quickly as possible. Therefore, it's best to always end your persuasive document on a conciliatory note. Invite your readers to respond as honestly and as directly as possible, and make it clear that—whatever they decide at present—you are still open to future negotiations on the subject.

14 WRITING WITH ENERGY

Good business writing is straightforward. Your readers will appreciate the truth, shared with simplicity by a writer who has given the topic attention and has decided what is important.

▶ USE A CONVERSATIONAL TONE

Good writing has the feel of a real person talking—warm, natural, and direct. Excessive formality makes your writing stilted and difficult to read. However, this doesn't mean that you should use slang, sarcasm, or little jokes. Find a balanced approach that is appropriate for your audience.

A great technique for developing your own voice is to read your work aloud. If you do it regularly, you'll begin to notice when other voices are intruding or when you are using roundabout phrases. In time, your sentences will gain rhythm and force. Reading aloud helps you to remember that, when you write, you are, after all, telling something to somebody.

Keep these questions in mind:

- Am I saying this in plain English?

- Are these words that I normally use?

- Am I saying what I know to be true instead of avoiding the real issues?

▶ BE DIRECT

Avoid confusion; say what you mean.

Use Personal Pronouns (*I, We, You*) Whenever You Can

Confusing: The main order of business was taken under discussion before a vote was held on the four proposals.

Direct: We discussed the main order of business and then voted on the four proposals.

However, do not hide behind *we* when you really mean *I.*

Tell What Something Is, Rather Than What It Isn't

Confusing: He's not often on time for meetings.

Direct: He's usually late for meetings.

Confusing: The installation does not meet our specifications.

Direct: The wallpaper is mismatched in two corners, and a number of bumps are visible on the south wall.

Use Direct Questions

Replace implied questions with direct ones and your writing will sound more like a real conversation. An added bonus is that you will often get real information from your readers.

Indirect: We welcome your comments.

Direct: Do you have any comments? If so, please let us know.

Indirect: Please determine whether we are responsible for undelivered back orders.

Direct: Are we responsible for undelivered back orders? Please let us know.

▶ CHOOSE ACTIVE VERBS WHENEVER POSSIBLE

You can write a verb in active or passive voice. Active is direct, passive more roundabout:

Passive: An inspiring talk was given at the luncheon.

Active: Greta Schultz gave an inspiring talk at the luncheon.

Sometimes, the passive voice is necessary—when you do not know or are not at liberty to say who is doing the action.

Passive: A pedestrian was struck down at the intersection.

However, business writers sometimes use the passive voice because they think it sounds more "objective" and "official." It also sometimes has the advantage of hiding responsibility or softening harsh news.

> *Passive:* Mr. Theron Smith's position has been terminated effective Monday, April 16.

More often than not, you can put energy into your writing by converting passive verbs into active ones whenever possible.

> *Passive:* A one-day writing skills workshop will be planned by the in-service committee.

> *Active:* The in-service committee will plan a one-day writing skills workshop.

▶ Get Rid of *Being* Verbs

Being verbs, like *is* and *are,* sap the energy from your writing. They dilute your sentences.

Look out for *am, is, are, was, were, be, being, been.*

Especially watch out for *there is, there are, there were, it is, it was.*

Often you can replace *being* verbs with forceful verbs. Sometimes you will have to rewrite or combine several sentences.

> *Passive:* It is important that we examine the future implications of merging these departments.

> *Active:* We must examine the future implications of merging these departments.

> *Passive:* The presentation was well received. The client was particularly impressed by the design of the logo.

> *Active:* The client loved the presentation—particularly the design of the logo.

Whenever you can, replace limp verbs with dynamic verbs. The changes will energize your sentences.

15 Trimming Wordiness

Often we think that people are impressed by a writer who uses big words and long sentences. Actually, people are more impressed by a writer who is *clear*.

▶ Minimize Jargon: Replace Fancy or Technical Words

Within a specialized field, technical terminology has its rightful place. It can save time and effort because it is instantly recognizable by the people within that field. However, even when you are addressing other specialists, jargon can easily become confusing as well as boring; so strive to use everyday words as often as possible.

For example, replace

utilize with *use*	*necessitate* with *need*
conceptualize with *conceive*	*altercation* with *disagreement*
concur with *agree*	*interface* with *connect*

Jargon: With the reception of the new equipment, we will be enabled to conceptualize at least fifteen scaled drawings per day and thus gain a competitive edge against our competitors.

Clear: When we receive the new equipment, we can produce at least fifteen scaled drawings per day and outperform our competitors.

When you do use a technical term for a general audience, be sure to define or explain it.

As land becomes more scarce, the field of hydroponics—the science of growing plants in liquid—will create many new career opportunities.

▶ Delete *That* and *Which* Wherever You Can

Elmo is the monster that most four-year-olds prefer.
Elmo is the monster most four-year-olds prefer.

The budget which I am submitting will cut costs by 10%.
The budget I am submitting will cut costs by 10%.

▶ Omit Words That Sound Good but Carry No Clear Meaning

really	thing/something	proceeded to
absolutely	the fact that	shows a tendency to
wonderful	bring to a conclusion	is a person who
experience	at this point in time	in today's society
personality	with the result that	come to terms with
situation	expresses an opinion that	

Wordy: The reason Ms. Pawatti resigned was due to the fact that she was sick.

Trim: Ms. Pawatti resigned because of illness.

Wordy: In today's society, uncertainty is something we all fear.

Trim: We all fear uncertainty.

▶ Avoid Redundancy—Pointless Repetition

Wordy: She gave birth to her baby at three a.m.

Trim: She gave birth at three a.m.

Wordy: The work counters are creamy beige in color and coordinate with the appliances.

Trim: The beige work counters coordinate with the appliances.

Wordy: Ms. Moffet does not seem able to have the personal authority required for this position.

Trim: Ms. Moffet lacks the personal authority for this position.

When you trim, don't worry that your writing will be too short. If you need length, add examples and further thoughts. Look at the topic from a different viewpoint. Add points, not just words.

16 VARYING YOUR SENTENCES

The same idea can be expressed in many different ways, and every sentence has movable parts.

To improve your style, try reading your writing aloud. When you come across choppy or monotonous sentences, use some of the following techniques.

► WRITE AN IMPORTANT SENTENCE SEVERAL WAYS

You can turn a sentence that troubles you into a sentence that pleases you. Instead of fiddling with a word here and a word there, try writing five completely different sentences—each with the same idea. One could be long, one short, one a generalization, one a picture, and so forth. Often, you'll find that your first isn't your best. If you play with several possibilities, you'll come up with the one you want. This technique works especially well for improving introductions and conclusions.

► USE SHORT SENTENCES FREQUENTLY

Short sentences are the meat and bones of good writing. Intersperse short sentences throughout your writing for clarity and strength.

- They can simplify an idea.

  All in all, the plan failed.

- They can dramatize a point.

  No one in the room uttered a protest.

- They can add rhythm.

  Everything went haywire. The lights blew. The alarm started screeching. Water spewed from the sprinkler system.

- They can be blunt and forceful.

  Another salary review is definitely in order.

If you're getting tangled in too many words, a few short sentences will often get you through.

▶ Lengthen Choppy Sentences

Using only short sentences, nevertheless, can make your writing monotonous. If you want to lengthen a sentence, the simplest way is to add concrete information.

> Gina Popovic is our strongest editor.

> By signing prolific and popular authors, Gina Popovic has built the Female Private-Eye series into our strongest book list.

▶ Combine Choppy Sentences

Combine two short sentences back-to-back. Here are three ways:

- Put a semicolon between them. (Be sure each half is a complete sentence.)

> We are considering the use of heat pumps for this project; an alternative might be solar panels.

- Put a comma followed by one of these connectors:

but	and	so	yet
for	nor	or	

> We are considering the use of heat pumps for this project, but an alternative might be solar panels.

- Put a semicolon followed by a transition word and a comma. Here are the most common transition words.

however	for example	meanwhile
therefore	furthermore	nevertheless
instead	in other words	on the other hand
besides		

> We are considering the use of heat pumps for this project; however, an alternative might be solar panels.

▶ Combine Sentences to Highlight the Major Point

Often, sentences contain two or more facts. You can show the relationship between these facts so that the most important one stands out.

In these examples, two ideas are given equal weight.

> I recommend that we reconsider the February deadline. The ice storm has delayed everyone here.

> The small yellow tomatoes are difficult to obtain. Joe Dunn promises to deliver a bushel each week.

Here are the same ideas with one point emphasized.

> I recommend that we reconsider the February deadline because the ice storm has delayed everyone here.

> Even though small yellow tomatoes are difficult to obtain, Joe Dunn promises to deliver a bushel each week.

Notice that the halves of these sentences can be reversed.

> Because the ice storm has delayed everyone here, I recommend that we reconsider the February deadline.

> Joe Dunn promises to deliver a bushel of small yellow tomatoes each week—even though they are difficult to obtain.

Usually the sentence gains strength when the most interesting point comes last.

▶ Insert the Gist of One Sentence Inside Another

The problem with most choppy sentences is that one after another starts with the subject of the sentence. Sometimes you can use *who* (for people) or *that* or *which* (for things) to start an insertion. Sometimes you can reduce the insertion to a word or phrase.

> The PS/2 port is at the back of the laptop. It can be used to connect an external mouse or a keyboard.

> The PS/2 port, which is at the back of the laptop, can be used to connect an external mouse or a keyboard.
>
> The PS/2 port, at the back of the laptop, can be used to connect an external mouse or a keyboard.

To stress the most important parts of your sentence, tuck in interrupters or insertions. Put transitions or minor information into the middle of your sentence.

> He procrastinates, as we all have observed, yet always meets his deadline.
>
> From my point of view, however, that's a mistake.
>
> The concrete, for example, was of poor quality.

Remember to put commas on both sides of the insertion.

▶ USE PARALLEL STRUCTURE

Parallel structure—repeating certain words for clarity and emphasis—makes elegant sentences.

> To be honest is not necessarily to be brutal.

In a list of parallel items, save the most important one for last.

> We are prepared to offer you continuation of your health insurance for two years, the use of your office and secretary for two months, and 250 percent of your current annual salary.

Famous quotations are often based on parallel structure.

> I came, I saw, I conquered.
>
> —Julius Caesar

> To believe your own thought, to believe that what is true for you in your private heart is true for all men—that is genius.
>
> —Ralph Waldo Emerson

> Ask not what your country can do for you; ask what you can do for your country.
>
> —John F. Kennedy

For the correct usage of parallel structure, see Chapter 17, "Avoiding Tangled Sentences."

▶ Imitate Good Writers

Take a close look at the writings of some of your favorite authors.
A good exercise is to pick out a sentence or a paragraph that you
particularly like. Read it aloud once or twice; then, copy it over
several times to get the feel of the language. Now, study it closely
and try to write an imitation of it. Use the sentence or paragraph as a
model, but think up your own ideas and words. This exercise can
rapidly expand your ability to vary your sentences.

17 AVOIDING TANGLED SENTENCES

Look at your sentences to make sure that the parts go together.

ERRORS IN PARALLEL STRUCTURE

Strong sentences often use a list or a pair; the parts must be in the same format.

> *Parallel:*   Coming to terms with a problem is not always the same as coming to terms with its solution.

> *Parallel:*   Thalia recommends that we increase the budgets for print advertising, for new logo designs, and for calling former customers.

> *Not parallel:* Ms. Bronson could always be relied upon to meet her deadlines, to develop creative solutions, and always provided a fresh perspective on relationships with our clients.

Here, two verbs have *to,* but the last has no *to* but instead, an *-ed* ending. The first and last phrases have *always,* but the middle one doesn't.

> *Parallel:*   Ms. Bronson could always be relied upon to meet her deadlines, to develop creative solutions, and to provide a fresh perspective on relationships with our clients.

> *Not parallel:* First, assemble all ingredients: butter, sugar, baking powder, and eggs, and don't forget to sift the flour.

Here, all the parts of the list should be nouns.

> *Parallel:*   First, assemble all ingredients: butter, sugar, baking powder, eggs, and sifted flour.

Parallel structure is especially important when composing headings, a bulleted list, or items in a résumé. For example, the headings in this chapter are all nouns or noun phrases; in Chapter 10,

"Proofreading," the headings are all directions (imperative verbs begin all of them); in Chapter 6, "Paragraphing," the first two sets of bullets are sentences and the third set all nouns. The point is that within any group you must be consistent.

▶ Danglers

There are two problems. In one, a word (often a pronoun) has been left out, so that the introductory phrase doesn't fit with what follows.

> *Dangler:* Having won three design awards, the commission to renovate the post office was an additional accolade.

This sounds as if the commission won the awards. To correct it, add the missing word or words.

> *Correct:* Having won three design awards, the architects considered the commission to renovate the post office an additional accolade.

> *Correct:* The architects had already won three design awards; the commission to renovate the post office was an additional accolade.

The second problem occurs when a phrase or word in a sentence is too far from the part it goes with.

> *Dangler:* A former Congressional aide, our company found Brenda Shears to be a skillful leader.

This sounds as if the company is a former Congressional aide.

> *Correct:* A former Congressional aide, Brenda Shears has proved to be a skillful leader in our company.

▶ Mixed Sentence Patterns

Sometimes you start with one way of getting to a point, but one of the words slides you into a different way of saying it. The two patterns get mixed up. Correct a mixed sentence pattern by using one pattern or the other.

Mixed
(Incorrect):   By using our innovative program allows smooth integration of email and office files.

Here the writer started to say "By using our innovative program, you can integrate email and office files," but the phrase *innovative program* took over.

Correct: Using our innovative program allows smooth integration of email and office files.

Mixed
(Incorrect):   In the Republic of Cameroon has over 200 local languages.

Correct: The Republic of Cameroon has over 200 local languages.

Correct: In the Republic of Cameroon, over 200 local languages are spoken.

Note that, most often, these problem sentences begin with *by* or *in*.

18 ELIMINATING BIASED LANGUAGE

Biased language includes all expressions that demean or exclude people. To avoid offending your reader, examine both the words you use and their underlying assumptions.

▶ OFFENSIVE WORD CHOICES

Some wording is prejudiced, impolite, or outdated.

Eliminate name-calling, slurs, or derogatory nicknames. Instead, refer to groups by the names they use for themselves. For example, use women (not girls), African Americans (not colored people), Asians (not Orientals).

Replace words using *man* or the *-ess* ending with nonsexist terms. For example, use flight attendant (not stewardess), mechanic (not repairman), leader or diplomat (not statesman), humanity (not mankind).

▶ FALSE ASSUMPTIONS

Some statements are based on hidden biases. Look hard at references to any group—even one you belong to. Check for stereotyping about innate abilities or flaws in members of a group. After all, every member of the group does not believe, look, or behave exactly like every other member. For example, all women are not maternal, all lawyers are not devious, all Southerners are not racist, and all Japanese are not industrious. Many clichés are based in stereotypes: *absent-minded professor, dumb jock, Latin temper.*

Check assumptions that certain jobs are best filled by certain ethnic groups or one sex. For example, all nurses aren't women; all mechanics aren't men; all ballet dancers aren't Russian.

Watch for inconsistency.

- In a pair:

    man and wife

Instead, use

man and woman   or   husband and wife

- In a list:

two Republicans, a Democrat, an Independent, a woman, and an African American

This list assumes that everyone is a white man unless otherwise specified. Instead, use

three Republicans, two Democrats, and an Independent

▶ Faulty Pronoun Usage

Check pronouns for bias.

Each judge should have his clerk attend the conference.

- One option for revision is to use *his* or *her.*

Each judge should have his or her clerk attend the conference.

- A better solution is to use the plural throughout.

The judges should have their clerks attend the conference.

- Often, the most graceful solution is to eliminate the pronoun.

Each judge should have a clerk attend the conference.

You can find more help with pronoun choice in Chapter 43, "Consistent Pronouns."

PART

THREE

SPECIFIC BUSINESS WRITING

19 EMAIL AND FAX MESSAGES

Distinguish between the more formal messages that may be retained on file and the casual ones sent between colleagues.

Before you click "send," remember that innocuous little messages (as the writers initially considered them) can later turn up in lawsuits.

COMPLETE IDENTIFICATION

Every fax and email should make it easy to reply in other ways. If your email program doesn't have it, make a form that you can copy to the bottom of every business message you send. Use a similar form or your letterhead for faxes. Include the following:

- Your full name and title

- The company name and mailing address

- The phone, fax, and email numbers—including area codes (plus country codes for international correspondence)

- The name and number of the person to contact regarding this message if different from you

If your fax program doesn't do so, give the total number of pages with the phrase "including this page."

THE SUBJECT LINE

The subject line for a fax should give enough information that the recipient won't have to consult all your previous correspondence in order to respond.

The subject line for email needs to be short because many programs show only a few words as the new mail arrives. However, it still needs to be accurately phrased. There's nothing worse than learning that your urgent message was saved for evening reading because the recipient didn't know it was important.

Revise the automatic repetition of the original email subject line if necessary to be clear when you reply to someone's message. Come up with a pithy line that suits your current message. Abbreviate if you have to.

Urgent—from Kenneth

Re: Mont. fishing article

Change in NYer deadline

KEEPING THE MESSAGE BRIEF

A focused message that matches the subject line is easy to respond to quickly and to find later. If you are writing a lengthy, complex message, consider sending it as an attachment.

- Treat only one subject per email. When covering several topics, separate them into several emails for the sake of easier filing and easier reading.

- Give essential information up front. When referring to a previous communication, recap the highlights. If your email program automatically copies the entire original message into a reply, copy the relevant section into a clean email form.

- Use bullets and headings to make points easy to grasp.

- Trim unnecessary explanations and details.

SALUTATION AND COMPLIMENTARY CLOSE

Use the format for letters or memos for fax messages; however, the etiquette for email is still evolving. Here are your choices:

- You may omit both the greeting and the closure—as memos do—but most people don't, because it feels abrupt.

- You may begin and end as with a letter. For business communication—especially with strangers—it is preferable to retain the formalities.

Dear Ms. Fayla:

Truly yours, Tina Stone

- You may use a casual tone—appropriate with colleagues and established business acquaintances.

  > Dorothy—
  > Good Morning, Nathan!

  > Best, James
  > Talk to you Thursday. Samantha

DOUBLE-CHECKING BEFORE YOU SEND

Compose an important message offline on your word-processing program where you can make corrections easily; then paste it into your email.

In any case, read the message carefully—at least twice.

COPIES

Copy the message only to those who need to know. Most people resent having to go through excessive messages, and some also do not want their email addresses sent out wholesale. Don't put colleagues on the spot by copying higher-ups unless you mean to do so.

BLIND COPIES

With blind copies, those recipients and their addresses are not listed on the other recipients' copies, allowing for privacy. You can also send a blind copy to yourself—handy when you are sending the message from a different computer and want to retain a copy of the message.

ATTACHMENTS, JOKES, GRAPHICS

Send attachments, jokes, and memory-hogging graphics only if you're sure the person wants them.

Unless you are sure that recipients share your programs, ask them to let you know if they have trouble opening attachments.

Send attachments in rich text format (RTF) or as a portable document file (PDF), which will retain most of the formatting.

FORWARDING

Forwarding email is a fast and easy method of keeping others informed or delegating a task. However, because forwarding is frequently abused, many people delete forwarded messages without reading them. Therefore, before pressing the "forward" button, you may want to take these precautions:

- Ask recipients if they want such messages.

- Unless it is implied, get permission from the sender.

- Verify the accuracy of the message. See the appendix of this book for the addresses of websites that list virus hoaxes, urban legends, and scams.

- Check the subject line. If you've added your own note, you may want the subject line to more accurately reflect your message.

- Unless it is necessary for context (for example, when forwarding email to someone else who will then respond), copy only the relevant parts of the message (surrounded by quotation marks or >> <<) into a clean email.

- Except when you need to list who is getting the same information, use blind copies so that you are not broadcasting the email addresses of others.

ALTERNATIVE EMAIL SERVICES

Several services—for example, Yahoo and Hotmail—offer free email. It's a good idea to have an alternate email account in addition to the one your Internet service provides, so you always have another route for communicating. In addition, many people like to use different email addresses for personal, business, and purchasing correspondence. You can register your various email addresses at http://mail2web.com/, where you can then read your email from any computer.

MAINTAINING YOUR FILES

If your email program doesn't allow you to organize your messages into folders, copy and paste important messages into your word-processing program where you can organize them.

Work out a system for deleting or keeping important messages. As they arrive, print out messages you need to keep on file or use to draft a response. See Chapter 11, "Staying on Top of the Paper Flow" for further suggestions.

20 MEMOS

Memos are best for routine communications with colleagues—either in-house or to outsiders with whom you've established a business relationship.

Memos can range in tone from the very formal to the casual, but they are always more impersonal than a letter. Whenever you need to communicate any kind of sensitive or confidential information, always use a letter instead of a memo.

▶ FOLLOW THE STANDARD FORM

HEADING

If you are not using a standard company memo form, devise a form that you can use and keep it stored in your computer. It should include the following, in this order:

- The full name of the company—and the address, for memos going outside the company

- The name of your department, if applicable

- The phrase "Interdepartmental Memorandum" (for memos outside your department) or "Intradepartmental Memorandum" (for memos within your department)—if appropriate

- The line indicators in boldface (which are then filled in for each new memo)

  Date:

  To:

  From:

  Subject:

BASIC ELEMENTS

Date Give the complete date, including the year. Abbreviations or all digits are acceptable.

12/3/05   12.3.05   Dec. 3, 2005   3 Dec. 2005

To List only those who are directly affected by the memo (as opposed to those you just need to inform). Give full names; give titles only if necessary for informing recipients who may not know some of the others.

From Give your full name; title; phone, fax, and email numbers. Initial the final copy, in ink, right next to your name.

Subject Give as complete a description as possible, briefly worded.

> Subject: Breakfast meeting for all associates 7:45 a.m., Monday, 10/17/05 in T545—Honoring Annual Performance
>
> or
>
> Re: Arizona filming delayed two weeks, revised schedule below

Body Keep paragraphs short. If you have written your subject line accurately, the rest of the memo need be only briefly informative or persuasive. If your message is complicated, use bullets or headings to break out key points. Attach agendas or schedules if necessary.

> The Desert 667 shoot scheduled for 10/3/05 has been rescheduled for 10/17/05.
>
> Model injured.
>
> Ms. Navidovovitch twisted her ankle. Her physician expects her to be fully recovered by our new deadline.
>
> Donkey wrangler is reneging on the contract.
>
> We have found a substitute burro—contract has been signed. Legal department has been given all details on the donkey.
>
> All other personnel and arrangements are in place.
>
> I assure you that all crews and equipment are ready for 6 a.m. MDT, 10/17/05—according to the newly updated contracts.
>
> Confirming paperwork is en route via separate correspondence.

Closure Do not use a complimentary close with memos—as you would with letters. You may use a brief closing remark as a conclusion.

Thank you for your attention to this matter.

Thursday's meeting will enable us to resolve the final details for the Harvest Festivities.

I will be in touch with everyone by Monday morning.

Signature Sign or initial beside your name on the *From* line. Do not add a signature line at the end of the memo (appropriate only for a memorandum of agreement or a formal letter).

Copy list (optional). List the names and titles of persons who will be sent copies of the memo. If they are not at your address, give their addresses as well. Keep this list as short as possible—on a need-to-know basis.

> cc: Patsy Turner, Legal Dept.
> Sarah Miles, Accounting Dept.
> Spencer Hart, Jennifer Greene, Television Production Dept.
>
> Mike Rogers Agency
> 1667 West 28 Street, Suite 20
> New York, NY 10121/Tel. 212-555-3434

When you send the copies, highlight or check the name of the appropriate recipient.

Enclosure reminder (optional). If you have included additional documents, use the simple abbreviation *encl.* and an itemized list if there are several.

> encl.: revised production schedule
> revised contracts—to Legal Dept. only

▶ MEMORANDUM OF UNDERSTANDING

A document in the memo format may serve as a contract, binding on both parties once they have signed below the description of their agreement. In this case, the document is titled "Memorandum of Understanding" or "Memorandum of Agreement"—without quotations marks, italics, or underlining. The memo is addressed to the business affiliations of the signatories and is sent from the individuals who signed. Here you do use signature lines and date of signing. Do not initial the *From* line.

21 LETTERS

Take time to compose a few basic letters that reflect your own personal approach and that sound like you.

Most business writers send out a few standard letters—over and over. There are templates (providing design and layout) in most word-processing programs—and even letters to copy. Unfortunately, the rest of the business world has access to those same standard letters. If you develop your own templates, including key sentences, all you'll have to do is change a few details for a personalized letter.

▶ FOLLOW THE STANDARD FORM

HEADING

If you are not using your company's letterhead, make a heading that you can copy to the top of each letter. It should include the following, attractively arranged (usually centered or aligned at the left, but it is also acceptable to arrange across the top of the page), in this order:

- Full name of the company
- Street address with suite or room number if appropriate
- City, state, and zip code (plus country for foreign correspondence)
- Phone, fax, and email numbers

TYPEFACE

- Ordinarily, use a No. 12 easy-to-read typeface, such as Arial or Times New Roman.
- Do not use all capital letters or all italics.

SPACING

- Use an inch to an inch-and-a-half margin on all four sides.

- Single-space each part of the letter (addresses, paragraphs, copy list), but double-space after each part, including the date and salutation. In a short letter, you can skip four or six lines after the date.

- Indicate the beginning of each paragraph by skipping a line and starting at the left margin (block format).

- Justify (line up the margin) only on the left. Justifying both margins distorts the spacing between letters and words, making the letter harder to read.

- Check vertical spacing in Print Preview after you have written your letter. With short letters, add additional space between the date and the recipient's address to provide a more balanced appearance on the page. Use the Shrink to Fit feature to avoid ending a letter with just a few words on the last page.

BASIC ELEMENTS

Date Give the full date without abbreviations.

> September 28, 2005 **or** 28 September 2005

Addressee Give the person's full name and title, followed by the complete address. If you do not have a person's name, be as accurate about the title as possible.

> Mr. Kevin Park
> Vice President of Marketing
> Stylish Resortware, Inc.
> 1223 Avenue of the Americas
> New York, NY 10021

Subject line (optional). Give a brief reference if it will simplify the opening sentence.

> Re: Account ZH 48972-89

> or

> Re: Ms. Liza Greene's Promotion

Salutation Unless you are on a first-name basis, use the person's last name, followed by a colon. If you do not have the name, use the title.

Dear Mr. Park:

or

Dear Vice President of Marketing:

Body Usually a letter contains two or more paragraphs. Keep paragraphs short for quick reading.

Second and subsequent pages The top right corner of each page after the first should contain an abbreviated title for the letter plus the page number.

L. Greene's Promotion, p. 2

Complimentary close Use one of the tried-and-true phrases.

Very truly yours,
Sincerely,
Best wishes,
Regards,

Signature space Your signature is necessary to authenticate the letter. Skip three to four lines after the complimentary close. Here you will write, by hand in ink, your usual signature—full name but without titles—unless you are on a first-name basis with the addressee. Do not underscore the signature line.

Typed line(s) with your full name and title

Joanna Blossom
Director of Human Resources

Copy list (optional). Skip a line and then list the names and titles of persons who will be sent copies of the correspondence. If they are not at your address, give their addresses as well.

cc: Ms. Veronica Brooks
Vice President of Production

Mr. Sam Chapin
Equal Opportunity Office
1254 Dupont Circle
Washington, DC 20015

When you send the copies, highlight or check the name of the recipient.

Typist's initials If you're typing a letter for someone else, give
that person's initials in capitals followed by a colon and then
your own initials in lower case.

JL:efh

Enclosure reminder (optional). If you have included additional
documents, use the simple abbreviation *encl.* and add an
itemized list if there are several.

encl.:   photocopy of resignation letter
photocopy of original application
photocopies of employment reviews, 1997, 2002

▶ Make Your Letter Easy to Read

BEGIN WITH THE PURPOSE OF YOUR LETTER

I am writing to report about the employment history of Ms.
Carrie Young.

Thank you for a very informative tour of your facilities.

This letter is a formal request for a change in the packaging you
use for our mushrooms.

BE CLEAR AND DIRECT

If you expect a particular outcome as a response to your letter, say
so—politely, but up front. Use *I* and *you.*

I expect your company to replace the entire 12/7/04 shipment,
which was damaged because of your driver's negligence.

BE BRIEF

Give only those details necessary to explain your points.

END ON A PLEASANT NOTE

I hope that we can come to a mutually beneficial agreement.

Yours is the most impressive portfolio we have ever seen. Congratulations!

Thank you for your personal attention to this matter.

▶ Use Informal Handwritten Notes When Appropriate

Many occasions in business require a more personal response—even with someone you know only in a business context. Use these guidelines when thanking someone for an entertainment or when expressing a personal wish (such as congratulations, sympathy, holiday greetings):

The note should be handwritten in ink. It can be brief and may be added to a short printed message on a card. It should be in your own handwriting—not an assistant's.

The note should clearly be from you. Make sure that your full name and complete address are legible—at least on the envelope. Make reference to your business association if the message will be out of context.

> Mr. Johnson—
>
> Our entire firm extends sympathy to you on the loss of your beloved wife. We have honored her memory with a donation to your neighborhood block association.
>
> With regards,
> Janice Darwin
> Sherman, Sherman, & Peña

> Dear Christine,
>
> Best wishes to you and your family on the arrival of Calvin David! These flowers are from everyone at HSW.
>
> Cordially,
> Jay

See the appendix of this book for sample letters.

22 AGENDAS AND MINUTES

Both agendas and minutes need to be brief and objective.

▶ AGENDAS

The written agenda focuses the purpose of the meeting and the topics you expect to cover. Even informal meetings can benefit from a written agenda, distributed ahead of time.

Use a memo. The subject line should contain all essential information:

- Who should attend

- The location

- The day(s) of the week

- The complete date(s)

- The beginning and ending times with a.m. or p.m. plus, if necessary, the time zone

> Subject: Meeting for all sales reps with Marketing Director
> Tuesday, Oct. 19, 2005, from 10 a.m. PDT till noon

If necessary, provide the purpose of the meeting in an opening line.

> This meeting will determine the feasibility of an employees' service center.

List the topics, beginning (if appropriate) with the approval of the minutes of the previous meeting.

If it will simplify the activities of the meeting, list reports from the chair, subcommittees, or other participants. Personally alert those reporting what their time limits will be.

List the most important topics first, in case time runs short and some items have to be postponed.

Attach a detailed schedule if this is to be a multisessioned conference.

Attach any informational materials so participants will have time to prepare for the meeting.

See the appendix of this book for a sample agenda.

▶ Minutes of a Meeting

FOR FORMAL MINUTES

- Provide a heading including the name of the organization or group, "Minutes" (without quotation marks), and the complete date of the meeting.

- Give the location, who presided, and the time the meeting began.

- List the full names of the participants—or the approximate number of attendees for a larger meeting.

- Organize by using the agenda as it was actually followed.

- When relevant, include a brief list of points covered during discussion of each agenda item. If the minutes will be circulated as a formal record among individuals who were not present, expand on each point so that the rationale for each decision is clear.

- List the decisions reached, if any, after each agenda item. If Robert's Rules were in effect, include who offered motions and amendments and whether they were carried or rejected.

- Because you are reporting, refrain from inserting your own opinions.

- Give the time of adjournment.

- Sign "Respectfully submitted" with your name and position.

FOR INFORMAL MINUTES

If you are asked to summarize a meeting or presentation you attended, highlight the most important points brought up in the meeting and the decisions reached. It's a good idea to include the location, date, and time, plus a list of the attendees.

23 INSTRUCTIONS AND DIRECTIONS

Break down instructions or directions into small, manageable steps—in the order they are to be followed. Give advice as you go.

▶ PROVIDE BACKGROUND INFORMATION

Tell your readers what they must know before they start:

- Describe the task to be accomplished.

    This is the best way to increase the speed of your new hard drive.

- Define all unfamiliar terms.

    Grommets are the metal rims that protect the holes where the tent poles will be inserted.

- List the necessary materials and equipment.

- Indicate the steps that must be taken in advance.

    You need to know how to back up your system registry.

- Explain how to prepare the work area.

- If necessary, tell how to dress appropriately.

▶ LAY OUT THE STEPS TO BE FOLLOWED

- Anticipate any possible misunderstandings.

    The ingredients listed in parentheses may be substituted without compromising the taste.

- Be careful not to combine steps or to assume that the reader will know something you haven't spelled out.

    Lubricate and clean all the gears prior to the next step.

- Use transitions to guide the reader from step to step:

    first   meanwhile   next   after   before   while   when   now

▶ Provide Intermediate Descriptions

Describe how the product will look at each stage or how the worker will know the step is successful:

> At this point, the grain of the wood should be visible, but not raised.

> Now, your sales figures should appear in the graph and in the box of totals for the year.

▶ Embellish Instructions with Advice

Explain why you suggest doing a step a certain way; include safety or health advice.

> To protect your hands and to ensure sanitation, wear clean, heavy-duty, rubber gloves while securing the jar lids.

▶ Check Your Instructions Carefully

With your instructions in hand, follow each and every step. Make changes in the sequence as necessary. Then ask a colleague unfamiliar with the process to follow the instructions. Pay close attention to any gaps. Revise where a step is unclear.

Note: Directions often depend on subtleties of language. If the instructions will be translated, consult native speakers of the respective languages.

24 REPORTS

Reports organize information, so they should be both easily understood and accurate. Tailor the content, tone, and length of a report to the intended audience.

Although a report needs to be complete, organize it to feature only the information your audience needs to know.

▶ AUDIENCE

Remember that your immediate audience may not be the only audience. Some reports are filed away and later surface in a performance review, a history of the company, or a court of law. Consider these implications as you write.

▶ PURPOSE

Reports are used routinely in business—and for a variety of purposes. Be conscious of what the report is expected to do.

- To pitch for an account
- To inform stockholders
- To record the decisions reached at a meeting
- To justify an action requiring approval

▶ TONE

Most reports (except for informal ones among colleagues) require a fairly formal tone. Keep some emotional distance; withhold your personal commentary for a section on recommendations or conclusions.

- Use people's last names and titles.
- Avoid slang, sarcasm, and anger.
- Imagine this report being read aloud to a group of people.

▶ Basic Elements

GENERAL FORMAT

If you are unfamiliar with the usual style for reports in your company or industry, check with colleagues to see a few samples. Of course, you need not be hidebound by what your predecessors have done, but often, continuity of style is expected.

Will the report require artwork? graphics? book binding, spiral binding, or a folder? Will it be published electronically? The visual presentation of the report affects its reception. Seek help if necessary.

TITLE PAGE

Make certain that all the basic information is prominently and attractively featured.

- Title
- Complete date, including year
- Company name (address may be on the back cover or on the second page)
- Prepared (or edited) by (your full name; title; phone, fax, and email numbers)

TABLE OF CONTENTS
(FOR REPORTS OF FIVE PAGES OR MORE)

List the section headings and page numbers; for lengthy reports, list subheadings as well.

THE REPORT ITSELF

Introduction (Think of this as "The Executive Summary.")

- Include necessary background or history.
- Be sure all the main points of the report are presented briefly.

Body Paragraphs

Often a report is written in response to a request. It is your job to organize the information so that the important points are featured.

- Make sure that any questions have been answered.
- Use facts and examples to demonstrate your key points.
- Use mostly short paragraphs.

Two typical organizational patterns are covered at the end of this chapter.

Headings

Headings should be inviting but also accurate. Do one check for outline logic after you have revised and reorganized the report. Break up lengthy sections with subheadings whenever possible.

Make sure that all headings are in similar grammatical format—for example, all nouns (such as in this chapter) or all verb phrases (such as in the previous chapter, "Instructions and Directions").

Graphics

Insert illustrations, charts, and graphics within the text at the point of reference. See Chapter 8, "Adding Visual Interest."

Conclusions and Recommendations

Highlight the most important points in your conclusion, and/or list recommendations for future action.

Appendix

Supplementary information, supporting illustrations, lists of sources consulted—all go at the end of the report, with an appropriate heading for each.

Index

Lengthy reports may need an index listing topics, names of individuals, and names of companies. Most word-processing programs have a feature that will give you a good draft of an index, which you can then edit.

► Electronic Versions

Make certain that you list the contents of even a short report at the beginning of an electronic version—preferably with links to each section so readers won't have to scroll through the entire document to reach the section they are interested in. Spend time on the formatting, design elements, and colors for the most attractive and easy reading possible. See the next chapter, "Websites," for further suggestions.

► Two Common Types of Reports

Here are two outlines you can apply to writing many reports.

STUDY OF A PROBLEM

- Give the historical background.

- Explain your methodology.

- List the findings in detail, but organized by type—such as "Problems due to poor drainage," "Problems due to inadequate sanitation," and so forth.

- Label examples as such.

- Give your recommendations.

- Attach a list of sources researched, if appropriate. If you used personal interviews, be sure to include the interviews in your list—names, positions, dates interviewed, and so forth. See Chapter 30, "Crediting Outside Sources."

DESCRIPTION OF ACCOMPLISHMENTS (COMPANY REPORT OR PERSONNEL REVIEW)

- Organize the accomplishments by type.

- Arrange the types in descending order of importance.

- Within each type, list accomplishments in chronological or hierarchical order.

- Find a unifying theme to use in the introduction and conclusion, and as transition between sections.

See Chapter 5, "Organizing Your Ideas," for suggestions on how to organize sections of the report.

25 Websites

Think about your audience when you design a website, and focus on the information you want visitors to get.

IDENTIFY YOUR MESSAGE

Before you set up your website, spell out what you hope to communicate.

- Who is your intended audience?

- What main points do you want to get across?

- What is the image you wish to promote?

USE A DESIGN THAT SUPPORTS YOUR MESSAGE

Don't let special effects interfere with your major points. Even if you are working with an experienced designer, keep in mind your goals of informing and persuading.

Organize the contents. Arrange your information so that visitors can easily find what they need.

- Feature the visuals that explain your main points.

- Use brief, clear headings.

- Break up large blocks of text, using subheadings and bullets.

- If you have more than a few parts, give a table of contents up front.

Make navigation easy. Both new and return visitors should be able to find what they want.

- Test your site to make sure that visitors won't get hung up at any point.

- Make it easy to bypass introductory or background information.

- If you can, use a sidebar with links to each section of your website.

- Supply a means to return to your homepage from any point within your website. Otherwise, add a warning so the visitor can bookmark.

- If you are providing links to other websites, make sure that they are active.

Avoid clutter. It's all right to be entertaining, but you don't want to distract visitors from your main offering. You don't need to fill every square inch of every page.

- With a text-dominant site, use visuals where they can add information or reinforce your point.

- With a predominantly visual site, add text only for clarity.

- Make sure that illustrations are large enough and appealing to the eye. Many small pictures can lead to clutter.

- Streamline biographies and histories of the company or project.

Create a tone and style that will communicate what you are—or are not—offering. For example, your music and graphics can tell the visitor whether to expect no frills or a more high-end service. In any case, be sure to provide a button for sound; some visitors logging on at work or the library may want to have a silent experience.

Provide options for visitors with disabilities. For example, http://bobby.watchfire.com/ will check your website pages for accessibility by the visually impaired. See the appendix of this book for other suggestions.

Keep "accidental visitors" in mind. Some who visit your site may be on their way elsewhere, but a pleasing site may invite them to return or refer you to others.

FEATURE ESSENTIAL INFORMATION

Make dates, locations, and prices easy to find. Often all the visitor wants to know is where, when, or how much.

- When referring to an event, give the precise location, day of the week, full date, and time—including a.m. or p.m. and time zone. This information should appear at the beginning of the announcement and should be modified once the event has taken place or is sold out.

- Give prices up front, indicating USD for "U.S. dollars" or a monetary conversion rate, if that applies. Also, make it clear when a price is negotiable; list any optional costs.

- Provide security for confidential transactions and display the appropriate symbol (a locked padlock). Offer alternatives for submitting credit-card information online.

Every page of your website should have your business name and preferred contact information—even when you also have a link to your email address.

- If appropriate, give your title or credentials.

- Indicate your affiliation if you are writing as a member of an organization.

- Give voice-mail or email addresses only if they will be checked regularly. Get technical advice so that any posted email address rejects spam.

- If you do not want to give the exact physical location of your business, at least give the city and state, region, or country.

Give references. If you have quoted someone or made claims about your work (awards won, comparisons to others), give the source information.

Add a copyright notice. Place © plus the date and your business name below any of your proprietary information and images.

Give the date of the latest revision of your website. Regularly updated websites indicate a business's careful attention to detail.

COORDINATE YOUR WEBSITE WITH YOUR OTHER BUSINESS MATERIALS

Strive for a consistent image in all your communications.

- Use the same design features for business cards, letterheads, and office forms.

- These materials, like your website, should be uncluttered, so you feature your message.

PROOFREAD, PROOFREAD, PROOFREAD!

A single error can destroy your credibility. Get help with the proofreading, and pay particular attention to headings.

If you are hoping for an international readership, test the website with people familiar with the respective region(s).

26 NEWSLETTERS AND PRESS RELEASES

The purpose of newsletters and press releases is to both disseminate information and enhance the company's image.

▶ NEWSLETTERS

Newsletters can serve as great promotional tools outside the company; in-house, they can inform, entertain, and encourage camaraderie. Sending copies of newsletters with a personal note can give a small organization a very large image. •

DEVELOP A RECOGNIZABLE FORMAT TO USE FOR EVERY ISSUE

- Make the title easy to read—test by photocopying in black and white.

- Provide all pertinent information—including the full name of the editor, the company name, complete mailing address, phone, email, and fax numbers—preferably in a border on the back page.

- Date and number each issue.

WRITE FOR YOUR PRIMARY AUDIENCE, BUT KEEP OTHERS IN MIND

- Check articles for context and tone—for example, outsiders may not get your "in" jokes.

- Provide background information where necessary for outsiders.

- Identify all persons by full title or job description.

- Invite response from your audience, especially on high-interest events. Then, publish appropriate letters—with the authors' permission.

USE INTERESTING LAYOUT

If you're new to layout, get some artistic advice on how to present your ideas visually and how to use the various tools available on computers.

- Use larger, bolder typeface for headlines.
- Use columns—three are best for 8½-inch pages.
- Use subheadings and borders.
- Break up articles so that features begin on the first page and continue on a later page.

KEEP ARTICLES SHORT

- For news articles, use the news lead—*who, what, when, where, how,* and sometimes *why*—in your opening sentence.

  On May 23, 2004, Mergentime broke ground for its new headquarters in Amarillo.

- Include feature articles highlighting individuals, departments, and projects.
- When rationales or explanations must be provided, set them off with a heading or border.
- Use photographs or drawings to add interest or explanation.

PROVIDE USEFUL INFORMATION
AND ANNOUNCEMENTS

Always include a "spotlight" story—a case history about a product or a feature on different individuals within the organization. People love to read about other people and also enjoy seeing their own names and pictures in print.

Include a calendar of upcoming events; announcements of births, weddings, and deaths in the families of employees; or interesting facts about the company's history, demographics, and successes. These items can fill blank spaces where columns run short—or you can add an attractive or entertaining graphic.

Also, don't overlook the opportunity to use the newsletter to gather information from readers—which you can then report about in a later issue. Most people appreciate a piece of informal research which they haven't had time to do themselves.

ELECTRONIC VERSIONS

If your newsletter is available online, provide a sidebar with links to each current article and to related articles from previous issues. Make sure that each article includes your publication's title, email and postal addresses, and the latest date of revision. See the previous chapter, "Websites," for further ideas.

▶ PRESS RELEASES

Press releases must be ready for publication. Broadcasters, local newspapers, and industry publications may be happy to use your release as is, so check every fact for accuracy; proofread thoroughly.

- Use the news lead—*who, what, when, where, how,* and sometimes *why.*

- Be brief. Editors may cut your last few paragraphs, so be sure the important information is up front. This arrangement (reverse pyramid) places less important information in each successive paragraph.

- Identify all individuals by full name and title or position.

- Provide background information and label it as such.

- Provide a press kit, if appropriate—a folder including photographs with captions, illustrations, fact sheets, and biographical information.

See the appendix of this book for a sample press release.

27 PROPOSALS

In a proposal you must convince your audience about the value of what you say—to persuade them to accept your point of view.

The proposal attempts to persuade a client, a funding organization, a supervisor, or a committee that your services or project will meet their needs—often within a specified budget.

▶ GENERAL GUIDELINES

ASSESS THE AUDIENCE

Be very clear about whether you're dealing with a receptive audience. If necessary, do some research to discover your best method for winning a positive response.

- What sorts of services are required?
- What sorts of projects has this audience supported in the past?
- Can you demonstrate a value that will persuade this audience? For example, will you provide a benefit that meets the goals of this audience?
- How are decisions made? Will the people evaluating your proposal follow a set procedure? Is one particular person crucial to the decision?

ADOPT A PROFESSIONAL TONE

Determine the approach that will win the respect of your audience.

- Use a style that is warm and natural without assuming friendship.
- Guard against sounding desperate, cute, or intimate.

For advice on strategy, see Chapter 13, "Writing to Persuade."

SEEK ADVICE

Be sure to solicit advice from colleagues who have written successful proposals in the past. Funding organizations often have staff members assigned to advise prospective applicants; take advantage of their assistance.

▶ BASIC ELEMENTS OF THE PROPOSAL

COVER LETTER (EXECUTIVE SUMMARY)

If at all possible, keep your cover letter to one page. The cover letter may be the only thing a busy executive ever reads. So make it brief but complete.

Opening paragraph Summarize in a few sentences the main points of the proposal.

- What are you proposing?
- Who will benefit? How?
- Who will be involved?
- How much will it cost?
- What is the estimated schedule?

Body paragraphs The middle of your cover letter will take the same points mentioned in the opening paragraph and briefly explain each. Use bullets or headings for each subtopic. Above all, remember that your goal is to persuade:

- Present the reasons why your proposal should be adopted.
- Summarize your supporting evidence.
- Highlight the most convincing facts.

Conclusion End with a summation of the benefits of the project and, if appropriate, your desire to undertake the project. Provide a list of the supporting materials you are attaching.

THE PROPOSAL ITSELF

Application forms If there is an application form that you must
use, scan it if an electronic version is not available. Pay close
attention to the guidelines because a technicality could
eliminate you from the competition.

If no format is prescribed A good outline would include the
following sections:

- Overview of the proposal
- Explanation of the problem—the goal of the proposal
- Proposed solution with factual support
- Logistics: timetable, personnel, budget
- Criteria for evaluating the project

SUBMIT THE MOST PERSUASIVE MATERIALS

Supporting evidence may include:

- A list and detailed description of all services that will be provided
- Reports of studies you or others have conducted
- Samples of previous work (portfolios, photographs, publications, videos, CDs, DVDs, websites)
- Tables, charts, diagrams
- Letters and memos from colleagues

For external proposals (to clients and outside funding agencies), also
include:

- Your résumé—and those of any colleagues who will be working with you
- Testimonials from previous employers or clients

For external proposals, you will need permission to reproduce
material taken from outside sources, adding "reproduced with
permission" after the credit line.

If you are submitting a proposal electronically, consider the advice
offered at the end of Chapter 24, "Reports."

28 RÉSUMÉS

Your résumé serves as an essential tool for job hunting; once you have a job, it can be modified for promotional purposes.

The résumé and cover letter attempt to persuade a very busy employer to grant you some precious time. Your reader wants to know what skills you have that will benefit the company.

Whether submitted electronically or on paper, both cover letter and résumé should make the level of your accomplishments clear, in a concise way. Save detailed documentation for the interview. If you lack experience in your chosen field, emphasize the relevant job skills you have developed.

Features of an appropriate résumé vary from field to field. Look at several résumés in your own profession for guidance.

Although the term *CV* (for *curriculum vitae*) is sometimes used instead of *résumé*, the two are not identical. *CV* refers to the detailed listing of experience in the academic or research professions, from education through work and publishing history. In the business world, use a résumé, as presented here.

See the appendix of this book for a sample cover letter and four sample résumés.

▶ COVER LETTER

In a job search, your résumé should always be accompanied by a cover letter (folded together, with the cover letter on top but not attached). Even if you decide to do a mass mailing as part of your search, each cover letter must be individually addressed (preferably to a name, not just to a title) and individually signed, in ink.

- The cover letter should be at most a page long. It should be readable in less than a minute.

- If you have a personal connection, mention it up front (and do everything possible to find a personal connection).

    James Stone recommended that I apply to you for the position of systems director.

- Stress how you will fit into this specific organization.

    My experience with all aspects of DataSystems technology qualifies me uniquely for supervising your planned expansion.

- Do not overlap your résumé point for point, but do stress your most important credentials for this position.

    As the enclosed résumé shows, I have shouldered increasing levels of responsibility in management information systems since earning my degree.

- Make clear your availability for interview or teleconference.

    I will be in Boston for the next two weeks at the numbers listed below, should you wish to discuss my credentials.

▶ Format of the Résumé

To ensure that your résumé will be retained, make it as brief and to-the-point as possible.

- If you can, keep your résumé to one page.
- Strive for an uncluttered, crisp look.
- List your work history by date, employer, and job title(s), with the most recent and the most impressive first. Do not list salaries.
- Feature your best points. Use headings, subtopics, and so forth.
- Make sure that headings and explanations are consistent in grammatical form and in style. See Chapter 17, "Avoiding Tangled Sentences."
- Offer to submit a portfolio or samples of your work or letters of recommendation upon request; unless they have been requested, do not attach references. Attach a photograph (head shot) only for the performing arts, entertainment, or fashion industries.

▶ Content

Your all-purpose résumé should be written so that it lists your job history. Then you can modify your résumé as needed to feature your skills and background according to the requirements of a specific position or for promotional purposes. See the appendix of this book for a sample résumé that has been modified to feature certain skills. This is the sort of résumé you would use when changing fields.

Heading At the top, either centered or arranged attractively, give your full name, complete home address, current business address only if appropriate, phone and fax numbers, and email address. If you are giving a pager number, indicate that fact in parentheses—and only list it if you are vigilant about returning calls.

Objective(s) Most of the time, you can omit the objective because it is implied in your application for that particular job. However, if it isn't, give a brief phrase or two describing your current career goal—if you can write one appropriate to this audience.

> **Objective:** to serve in a management position in the hospitality industry

> **Objective:** to affiliate with a progressive firm that will benefit from my skills as a senior architect and project manager

Reverse chronology of job history Beginning with your current job, list the dates, the name of the employer, and the job title. If the job title doesn't make the duties clear, explain them briefly, featuring the skills the prospective employer would require. Give a brief description of the company if it is not a nationally recognized one, or if you must refer to your current employer anonymously.

List of accomplishments or skills Within the list of your previous jobs, briefly describe your main strengths or outstanding accomplishments at each.

> **June 2003–present** (firm supplying the St. Louis area with personalized installation and service for intranets). On-site programmer and troubleshooter. Created, installed, and maintained personalized software for clients—many in high-data industries with systems of over 100 workstations.

Brief education history List by dates, university, and degree, followed by your major or type of study. If relevant, mention extracurricular activities. Unless you are trying to fill up the page, omit all reference to high school and earlier.

1997–2003 University of Vermont BS in Computer Technology. Dean's list. Volunteer 1999–2002 (three hours weekly, twelve weeks per semester, seven semesters) training senior citizens in computer use. Also provided maintenance to computer systems in village community center.

List of references Usually, it is best to end with "references are available upon request," but if you already have letters of recommendation, you can list the names and titles of the people who wrote the letters. You may also list the contents of your portfolio or other materials that support your credentials.

▶ ELECTRONIC SUBMISSIONS

Many companies prefer résumés in electronic format, so be sure to keep an updated file ready to send.

- Unless specifically requested not to do so, include a cover letter as the first page of your résumé.

- Make certain that your name and email address are on each page—perhaps as a header.

- Submit a single file, as an attachment to a very brief email that includes your contact information. Use PDF or RTF format.

- If you are given only a coded email address or a vague description of the employer, use an impersonal, respectful salutation in your cover letter—such as, "Dear Sir or Madam," "Dear Director of Personnel," or "Dear Engineering Firm."

- Unless you are certain that it is appropriate for this employer, do not add music or special effects to your résumé.

▶ THANK-YOU AND FOLLOW-UP LETTERS

It's not just good manners but also good business to thank your interviewer. If the interview was cordial and informal, you may wish to send a handwritten note on a tasteful card or plain note paper. In some circumstances, a thank-you in an email can be appropriate. However, a typed, formal thank-you letter is often the best choice. Your goal is to keep your name in consideration—if not for a job offer then perhaps for a later referral.

No matter which format and tone you use, make sure that your thank-you covers these points:

- Your gratitude for the time and consideration extended to you
- Your desire to join the organization and a brief summary of what you offer
- Comments related to the interview—praise for the interview and the organization
- An offer for further information about your qualifications
- A hope to hear from the company

If, after two weeks, you haven't heard from anyone at the company (and you know that the position remains open), send a short follow-up letter. Keep a positive tone, and include these points:

- Remind the interviewer that you are still interested.
- Summarize your qualifications.
- Thank the interviewer again for every consideration.

PART
FOUR

SPECIAL
PROJECTS

29 RESEARCH ON THE INTERNET

The Internet has made it quick and easy to find plenty of information on just about every topic. However, in order find the best information, you need to be focused during the process.

▶ GENERAL GUIDELINES

Whether you are looking for information to solve a problem or to include in a memo or report, you need to get and keep a clear idea of what you want to know.

BEFORE YOU PLUNGE IN

Jot down questions that can direct your research. Listing what you hope to discover reveals what you already know and where you need information. For example, you may need mostly statistics, or photos, or background. Or you may need a deeper level of information in just one aspect of your topic.

Think of who would know the answers. The most efficient research often begins with a query to the appropriate expert. If you can't ask the person, add that name and area of expertise to your list of questions. You need to know what the authorities have written or said.

Pull out some keywords to use. Develop a list of subtopics and synonyms that you can use as search terms in your research. For example, for a report on gas expenses, you might jot down the names of a few makes of cars, the phrases "fuel-efficient," "miles per gallon," "gasoline prices," and so forth.

AS YOU WORK

Remain open to discovery. Allow time to consider different perspectives—for example, technical vs. artistic, or traditional vs. avant garde, or management vs. labor. Often, a contradictory interpretation of the facts can increase your own understanding of them.

Be aware that the web can divert you. If you're not careful, you can easily get sidetracked by interesting but irrelevant information. Keep your initial questions in mind as you work, and skip material that doesn't give you answers.

Recognize dead ends. If you haven't found what you need among the first twenty-five results, rephrase the search or try a different search engine or website.

Delay careful reading. Use "find" (Ctrl + F) to identify paragraphs containing your keywords and read those to see if the coverage is appropriate. Skim and then save articles until you have gathered a variety from different sources.

Save material in folders. Label folders according to subtopics—both in your word-processing program (for files and notes) and in your browser (for web addresses). You might even designate a folder for off-topic, later reading.

Record the sources of information. Make sure that you know where you got each piece of information—"bookmark," save to file, or email key articles to yourself.

WHEN TO QUIT

You will need some time to organize the material you have discovered, to reflect on it, and perhaps to write it up for others. Writing a formal report almost always takes more time than the research.

▶ TIPS FOR SEARCHING

WHERE TO SEARCH

See the appendix of this book for descriptions and addresses of resources mentioned here, plus many others. The list of all resources will be regularly updated at http://www.writingshortcuts.com/.

Use several search engines. Most people begin by typing in a word or two with Google or Yahoo, and that may give enough information for a simple question. The same query will bring up different results from different search engines, especially if you use an "advanced search." You may also find that one search engine is better for your topic.

Metasearchers such as Search.com modify your phrases as needed to search simultaneously through a number of the most popular search engines and then organize the results.

Use specialized databases. The reference desk of your local library can tell you about specialized databases for your particular topic, and may allow comprehensive off-site access. Many databases for specific fields—such as *Medline* and *Findlaw*—are available online, some for a fee per article. Others—such as Lexis-Nexis, which indexes all news articles—are available only through libraries or paid subscription.

Consult research libraries. Some major libraries, such as the Library of Congress and the New York Public Library, have websites that you can consult—for listings of books and limited access to databases.

Scroll through reference pages. Librarians and other scholars have posted lists of resources, with descriptions and links to their websites—and each category is maintained by an expert in that field. Two of the most extensive reference pages are *Internet Public Library* and *Virtual Library.*

Consult homepages of colleges and universities. Most college websites provide links to their library and to course materials developed by college faculty: reading lists, syllabuses, and so forth. You can find these homepages through search engines. Try using the name of a particular college or your topic phrase plus "college."

Check websites of government agencies and nonprofit organizations. A wide variety of information is available from local, regional, and federal institutions. Use a search engine or consult a directory of associations. Look for websites with .gov or .org in their addresses.

Don't overlook other electronic media. National Public Radio, the Public Broadcasting System, and the commercial networks all maintain websites where you can get information on current events as well as features on a wide variety of topics.

Don't forget print materials. Many books that are out of print are now available online, such as those provided by the Bartleby Project. However, some information is not accessible electronically—in particular, many articles in print and the contents of most books. For thorough research, a trip to the library can provide important information available nowhere else.

HOW TO SEARCH

Use a subject directory. Most search engines provide subject directories, which are indexes that allow you to type in or click on a category and then on increasingly narrower subtopics. Since professional researchers have done the searching for you, typing *Movies!* in Yahoo, for example, quickly calls up a good selection of articles on movies.

Use a combination of search terms. Every search program uses slightly different rules of operation, but most allow you to enter more than one word to search. Check the directions or helpline of the program before beginning.

SEARCHING CONVENTIONS

- Quotation marks indicate that a phrase is to be treated as one search term—for example "Chrysler Building."

- "Boolean operators" such as *and* and *or* tell the search program how to interpret your list of terms. In general:

    and specifies that both terms should appear.

    or specifies that either term should appear.

    not specifies that a term should not appear.

    Some search engines use the plus sign (+) instead of *and*, a vertical line (|)—the uppercase of the backslash—instead of *or*, and the minus sign (−) instead of *not*.

When a search engine says that "Boolean *and* is implied," you don't need to type *and*; just type in all the terms you want with a space between them. For example, Google and Yahoo do not require *and*.

With some programs, you type your terms into separate boxes, labeled according to whether **this exact phrase, any, all,** or **none** of the words must appear.

Use phrases to provide context when a word has more than one interpretation. For example, "Maltese dog," "Catholic cardinal," "baseball diamond."

Use specific terms whenever possible. For instance, "Navajo rugs" rather than "Indian rugs."

For example, by using the following search terms in INfotrac (available in libraries), you can find basic information on community associations:

neighborhood and association and community and security not college

or

+neighborhood+organization+community+security-college

Different terms could be added if you wanted more information about community policing, neighborhood parties, urban block associations, and so forth.

PROBLEMS

The most common problems that researchers experience are that they can't find any sources or that they find too many. In either case, first consult the helpline for that search engine.

No Match for Your Request

• You may have misspelled one or more words.

• You may have used the wrong symbols or phrasing for that search engine.

- You may need to try a different search engine or database.

- You may have submitted too narrow a search. Try generalizing a bit. For example, try "teen and cell phone" rather than "teenage cell phone habits."

- Give both the abbreviation and the full name, linked by *or* (MSKCC or "Memorial Sloan-Kettering Cancer Center").

- Try adding more alternatives—both more general and more specific:

  chocolate, cocoa, bittersweet, "milk chocolate," mocha, Hershey's, Godiva

- The information may be there, but it is not available to you online—perhaps only to subscribers of a service, or under an obscure keyword. You may have to go to the library.

- The information may be there, but your service or theirs is overloaded. Try later.

Too Many Listings

Information can be buried (say in the 531st article that Google found for you).

- Take a look at the first ten results to see if they coincide at all with your topic. For instance, a query on *"eradicating moss in garden"* yielded thousands of articles with the first ten about garden stores selling moss. For articles on preventing moss, you will need to rephrase the search.

- If the first ten listings are on your topic, skim a few of them to extract more search terms.

- Add more words to your search string, putting a more specific word first.

HOW TO EVALUATE WHAT YOU FIND

In the spirit of the Internet, some very good information is published outside the conventional review and editing process. However, anyone can put up a website, and anyone can claim to be an authority. Use the following checklist to verify the information you plan to use. Above all, be careful about getting all your data from a single report.

Check the address. Foreign web addresses end in a two-letter country code (such as .ca for *Canada*). Web addresses in the United States end in a three-letter suffix. Use the web address as a reminder to check the approach to the topic.

.gov (government): Is there political bias?

.org (nonprofit organization): What does the organization promote?

.edu (educational institution): Is the author a professor or a student?

.com (business): Is the article selling or reporting?

.net (large network): Is the website supported by an institution or only by a private individual?

Also be wary of institutions that do not list their geographical address.

Check the credentials of the writer and sponsoring institution. When you encounter a page listing no author, business, or date, go to the root of the Internet address (deleting everything after the suffix, such as *.com*). Use a search engine or one of the directories listed in the appendix of this book to get details about the author and the organization.

Don't confuse information and aesthetics. An elegantly designed website does not guarantee accuracy of information. A poorly designed website may contain an impeccable report.

Check the date. Many topics require the latest information. There should be a "Last revised" date. Of course, every field has its "classics," and even outdated material may have historical relevance.

Examine the quality of the writing. Look for an objective tone, specific examples, footnotes or references, and careful analysis. Errors, other than an occasional typo, signal a lack of professionalism. Allow for the fact that English is the preferred language on the Internet, and some authors may not be proficient users of English.

Distinguish between primary and secondary sources. A secondary source is reporting or interpreting what someone else discovered. Often it helps to have analysis by an expert, but sometimes you need to see the originator's presentation.

Distinguish between opinion and fact. Watch particularly for manipulation of statistics. What does it mean when someone reports that the opponent "came in next to last" (in a two-person competition)?

Do not confuse popularity with accuracy. Check sensational "facts" by going to the complete source.

Check linkage. Do reputable websites link to this one? Does this website provide links to others of high quality?

Check for published corrections. Reputable news agencies publish corrections in a timely fashion—often on their website as well. In the appendix of this book, you will find additional help for checking facts and for identifying false stories on the Internet.

Ask an expert. Check a dubious claim by calling or writing someone in the field.

30 CREDITING OUTSIDE SOURCES

You can often improve a report or presentation by referring to the words or ideas of others. When you do, you will need to give credit.

Ordinarily you won't need to use the complex system required for documentation in college research papers. However, you will still need to identify the sources of quotations, facts, and someone else's original ideas. Crediting outside sources is more than a matter of honesty; it also:

- Lends authority to your assertions

- Demonstrates your thoroughness and knowledge

- Allows your reader to pursue the subject further

▶ IN-TEXT REFERENCES

The most graceful method for giving credit to a source is to mention the author, title, and copyright date within your sentence.

Book

> James Surowiecki, in *The Wisdom of Crowds* (2004), discusses how "collective intelligence" of groups can be used to solve a variety of problems. "In fact," he argues, "the more important the decision, the more important it is that it not be left in the hands of a single person" (222).

Notice that the page number, if you want to include it, goes in parentheses at the end of the quotation or the information, before the period. Should you prefer to put all the reference information into the parentheses, use the last name of the author and the date, followed by a comma and the page number.

> If you accept the conclusion that groups "genuinely were smarter than the smartest people within them" (Surowiecki 2004,190), giving decision-making power to small groups within the company makes sense.

Article

> Following David Allen's method, James Fallows says that he always has an electronic or paper notepad handy (*Atlantic Monthly* 2004, 173).

(Notice that the title of the publication is cited rather than the title of the specific article.)

Omit the page number for articles in newspapers, since page numbering may vary in different editions.

> Eilene Zimmerman reports that blogs are valuable sources of information for job seekers—and for employers (*New York Times*, November 3, 2004).

Internet

> Since 1984, the National Association of Town Watch has sponsored a National Night Out on the first Tuesday of August each year (http://www.nationalnightout.net/, Sept. 12, 2004).

The date given is the last update for the site, or if that is unknown, the date you viewed it.

When abbreviations are used in titles, provide the full name of an organization in square brackets. For long Internet addresses, use a brief form (such as one provided by Snipurl.com) or use a footnote.

> Mary Jane Gilhooley's article in *IAQ News* [*Indoor Air Quality News*] (March 12, 2003)[1] provides a good analysis of the benefits of live plants in the office.
>
> ---
>
> 1. http://www.iuoe.org/cm/iaq_greenbuild.asp?Item=447/.

▶ FOOTNOTES

You can use footnotes either for detailed identification of a source or for supplementary information. Footnotes are the least intrusive method of referring to sources, and word-processing programs make the formatting relatively easy.

You may use a footnote at the end of your report to refer to a single source you have used throughout. For multiple sources or for specific page identification of quotations or illustrations, use a series of footnotes (at the bottom of each page requiring a source identification) or endnotes (in a separate section at the end, labeled Endnotes, in regular font, without quotation marks). With footnotes or endnotes, begin with the number 1 and use a new number each time you cite a source. For each subsequent use of the same source, use the author's last name and the page number.

To identify a source, include:

- Author (first name first)—if no author is listed, put the organization that created the document.

- Title (for an article, include the title of the article, in quotation marks, and the title of the publication, italicized).

- Additional information, depending on the type of source.

  ~ For a book, the city of publication, publisher, and date

     1. James Surowiecki, *The Wisdom of Crowds* (New York: Random House, 2004), 222.

     2. Surowiecki, 190.

  ~ For an article, the date (and pages if you wish)

     3. James Fallows, "Personal File: Organize Your Life!" *Atlantic Monthly* (July-August, 2004), 173.

  ~ For a website, the date of last update (if available, otherwise, the date you viewed it) and the complete address

     4. National Association of Town Watch. "National Night Out," September 12, 2004. http://www.nationalnightout.net/.

▶ List of References Consulted

Using in-text references or footnotes should be sufficient to acknowledge sources in most business writing. However, on occasion, you may need or want to provide a list—labeled "Bibliography," "References," "Recommended Reading," "Works

Cited," or "Works Consulted"—at the end of a report. Depending on how you label it, this list can be used to acknowledge background research or the sources you have cited, or to give suggestions for further reading on the topic.

Use the same format as for footnotes. Do not number the list. Instead, put authors' last names first and make one alphabetical list. For each entry, indent the second and additional lines.

Note: This chapter presents a simplified version of the documentation styles recommended by the American Psychological Association, the *Chicago Manual of Style,* the Council of Biology Editors, and the Modern Language Association. Their web addresses and information on their style manuals are listed in the appendix of this book if you need to conform precisely to their individual specifications.

Bibliography

Fallows, James. "Personal File: Organize Your Life!" *Atlantic Monthly* (July-August, 2004), 171–76.

Gilhooley, Mary Jane. "Plants in the Workplace Have Been Proven to Improve Employee Productivity and Reduce Stress." *IAQ News* [*Indoor Air Quality News*], March 12, 2003. http://www.iuoe.org/cm/iaq_greenbuild.asp?Item=447/.

National Association of Town Watch. "National Night Out." September 12, 2004. http://www.nationalnightout.net/.

Surowiecki, James. *The Wisdom of Crowds.* New York: Random House, 2004.

Zimmerman, Eilene. "Before Applying, Check Out the Blogs." *New York Times*, November 3, 2004.

31 RECURRING PROJECTS

Much business writing falls into a few main categories and formats. Taking time to analyze how you produced what you have written makes it easier next time.

▶ DEVELOP TEMPLATES AND OUTLINES

Save yourself time by developing templates (basic layouts in your word-processing program) for all recurring written projects. Even projects that change substantially—depending on content and audience—may follow similar outlines or processes.

Review, for example, the various kinds of letters you regularly write. Select a few well-written ones so you can develop some templates that will work for you. You might identify these categories:

- Cover letter for contract
- Response to inquiry
- Response to proposal
- Response to job applicant
- Letter of recommendation
- Letter of complaint
- Letter requesting information

For each category, use the successful letter as your model, make a template, and label it accordingly. Make each template as detailed as possible, with as many key sentences and phrases as you can reuse.

You can develop a similar list for other types of writing you routinely do in the course of the year—such as annual reports, studies, evaluations, minutes, press releases, and so forth.

▶ KEEP A NOTEBOOK

As you work on a long-term or difficult project, take notes on the details of the process:

- The time schedule—particularly the length of time required by you and by others to complete each phase of the work
- The names, phone and fax numbers, and email addresses of consultants
- The reason for each success
- The reason for any difficulties
- The specific characteristics of this project and this audience
- Any cautions to yourself and others for next time

▶ Prepare a Tickler File

Using the details in your notebook, prepare a tickler file (a list of reminders keyed to a schedule) for each type of project. Include the following:

- A summary of the advice to yourself
- The phone/fax/email/address list of helpers and consultants
- Copies of the appropriate templates
- A copy of the last document
- A suggested basic schedule

32   LONG-TERM PROJECTS

Completing a long-term project on time requires that you identify your priorities for it early on and then methodically work on these priorities at regular intervals.

▶ PLANNING YOUR PROJECT

Brainstorm and Freewrite to Get a Sense of the Project

You should identify the following:

- The topics you will be covering

- The steps you must follow

- What you already have on hand

- The information you need and how you will get it

- The people you must call

- The additional supplies, reports, graphics, and so on that you need

- Any consultants, graphic artists, printers, and so on that you need to line up

Even procrastinators can do some initial planning. See Chapter 3, "Sizing Up Your Work Style." For tips on brainstorming and freewriting, see Chapter 4, "What to Do When You're Stuck."

Develop a Long-Term Plan for Your Project

- List the steps for the project in chronological order.

- Estimate the amount of time each step requires. Be very realistic—and generous—allowing time for delays and unforeseen disasters.

- Develop a series of deadlines for yourself—including time for some breaks.

- Make a schedule for any consultants, collaborators, or outside jobbers, and ensure their commitments.

Write a Tentative Outline or Table of Contents

Through your brainstorming and freewriting, develop a rough plan for the written product.

▶ During the Project

Keep a Notebook—Either on Paper or Electronically

Begin writing as soon as you can—out of order, any time that you think of something to say. In your notebook, keep copies of your schedule and your tentative outline, and revise them as necessary.

It's also a good idea to keep a section of your notebook just for notes to yourself. These notes should be about your sense of the project and where it is leading. Periodically, review what you have written and adjust the working document.

Make sure that you date each entry, and consider keeping a backup copy in a second location.

Network

Talk about your project with others. Over time, people can offer you information or advice if they think you'd welcome it. Schedule frequent meetings (at least by phone) with your associates, supervisor, or client. One problem with long-term projects is that they can be isolating. Discuss your project with friends—not so much to get their ideas as to articulate your own.

If You Need to Do Research, Begin Right Away

Gather information or conduct your study as soon as possible. Write up your findings as you go. Maintain a separate "clippings" file for the project and drop into it any bits of related information you might find useful at a later date.

Use Your Outline to Organize Files into the Computer

Using your outline or table of contents, name a file for each topic. As soon as you can, write a detailed outline, tentative notes, or a very rough draft in each file. What is important at first is to get something approximately close to what you want to say. Don't strive for perfection. You will expand or develop as you get further into the project.

Plan to Revise a Number of Times

- Put your work into a computer early in the process and store it in short documents rather than one long one.

- Large projects in particular go through more drafts than you might expect. Strive to have a rough draft of every part of the project by the time you are halfway through your allotted time schedule. Then revisit the parts to expand, revise, and fine-tune.

- Revision will entail not only touch-ups but complete changes of emphasis. Allow more time proportionately for revising a long project than you usually do for the revision process.

- Secure your files. Keep a second set off-site.

▶ AS THE DEADLINE APPROACHES

- Make sure that you have communicated whatever you require from others and that they are on schedule.

- Revise your outline if necessary and use it to format the entire document. Add headings and bullets so subtopics are clearly distinguished from main topics.

- Add a table of contents and index if needed.

- Go through the entire finished product several times, checking each time for just one aspect:

~ **Accuracy** Of facts, numbers, quotations, and so forth

~ **Completeness** No unanswered questions or unsupported assertions

~ **Readability** Plenty of headings, a layout that showcases your main points, brief paragraphs, and well-constructed sentences

~ **Correctness** Of grammar, punctuation, vocabulary, and so on

33 COLLABORATIVE PROJECTS

Collaborative projects require attention to teamwork as well as to the work itself.

▶ DEVELOP A FEW GROUND RULES

Decide on the division of labor. Be open to the variety of ways different people contribute. Talk over how each group member works and what each does best and likes to do. List all necessary steps and then let people volunteer. Make sure that the group reviews the final list so that everyone feels that the division of work is both fair and practical.

Decide on who will be speaking for the group. Designate one person as a contact or for follow-through with outsiders. This responsibility can be divided, but for example, the same person should be working with the graphics designer each time—and the group should agree on what will be said.

Decide how you will handle expenses. Unless your expenses will be absorbed automatically without outlay of either money or paperwork, agree on a list of expenses you know you will incur during the project and decide whether one person will act as treasurer or whether the group will review expenses periodically.

Agree in advance about how the group will handle conflict and disagreements. Negative criticism causes not only bad feelings but also poor work. Plan for any conflicts by agreeing ahead of time to immediately, openly, and honestly bring any problem before the group. Handle each conflict as it arises before it becomes severe.

Make sure that the group is functioning well—that no one is dominating and that no one is left out. People work at different rates. To work well in a group, it may be necessary to tolerate some degree of chaos. Exchanging news, having coffee, and arguing over the same point twice can be processes in becoming a team. Keeping in touch allows the group to work out any problems of procedure or content.

Be prepared to modify the original plan if it is not working.
For example, one member may have been working harder
and longer than anyone else with not much to show for it.
The group might decide that this person needs help or that
this part of the project needs to be reconsidered.

► USE TEAMWORK TO REVISE

Write separately, in most cases, and then come together. The
style and continuity are often disastrous when you compose
sentences together. Revise as a group, but recognize that good
revision takes time. The group needs to talk until you discover
what you really want to say.

Agree upon intermediate deadlines. Decide together when
everyone will bring a certain amount of work to discuss. Even
when you intend to divide the writing of the final report,
seeing one another's work at key points will help you to unify
the project and use everyone's ideas.

Use a system for working on interim drafts of the document.
Make sure that the date and time are on each draft and that it is
clear who has seen it. Develop a routing system—either the
same sequence for reading and reacting, or a schedule for people
to return their comments to one person who will collate them.

Circulate one copy of the final draft. Everyone should write
comments at the appropriate place in the document—always
identifying themselves by initials—either on the electronic
copy using markups, in colored ink on the page, or on sticky
notes.

Put one person in charge of the final manuscript. This writer
will make sure the style of different parts is consistent and
correct. A number of people should double-check the final copy.

34 THE SPOKEN WORD

Spoken errors are usually overlooked in conversations, but when you are giving a formal talk or presentation, be sure to keep your words error-free.

These suggestions apply to both broadcast and platform presentations:

- Be certain your grammar is correct—particularly subject-verb agreement and pronoun usage.

- Vary the rhythm of your sentences.

- Use active verbs.

- Use concrete language.

- Stay away from phrases that are offensive, sarcastic, or trendy. If in doubt, don't say it.

- Make contact with your audience and with other participants.

▶ PREPARATION

Prepare an outline with brief reminders of examples or anecdotes. As extra preparation, consider writing out an important speech in its entirety. In some cases, you may need to provide a copy for the record anyway, and writing it out helps you to craft better sentences. Read it aloud for practice, but remember to use the outline for your presentation.

Don't plan to read your speech. If you must have the entire speech with you for a sense of confidence, boldface and enlarge the headings so you can glance at them and extemporize on the details. You'll kill your presentation if you face your notes instead of your audience.

Practice your speech. You may find it helpful to stand in front of a mirror. Picture your audience—including any specific people you know. Enunciate clearly. Note where you stumble over the phrasing and simplify those parts. Use plain English.

Practice with any visuals you intend to use. Mark the points in the outline of your speech where you will be using the visuals. If possible, practice with the exact equipment you will be using.

Time yourself. Allow for whatever your habit usually is—do you speed up or slow down when onstage? Mark on your outline what points you can cut or expand upon—depending on how your allotted time is going. Especially in a broadcast, you cannot come up too short or go beyond your time limit. Planning ahead will prevent sudden panic.

▶ PRESENTATION

Bring a list of key points. Highlight the points you want to cover, and arrange them in order of importance. If others are controlling the agenda, make sure that your most important point is addressed as soon as appropriate.

Dress appropriately. Avoid complicated patterns and garish or noisy jewelry.

Insert a slight pause before you talk. For broadcasts and teleconferences, this regular pause will allow for any lag in transmission time. It also gives you an advantage when you need to pause in response to a tough question; the pause will be part of your rhythm.

Take brief notes (in one or two words) during the discussion in a platform panel or teleconference. This way, you can modify your planned presentation in reaction to others. Panel presentations and teleconferences—even formal ones—should operate as conversations.

Don't interrupt others—no matter how tempting. Even if you're correct in what you say, you will draw unfavorable attention to yourself.

Don't read!

35 EDITING OTHER PEOPLE'S DRAFTS

Whether you are collaborating or supervising, there may be times when you must offer advice on how to improve a draft.

▶ ASSESSING THE DOCUMENT AS A WHOLE

Before you read the document, determine the time available for making changes and assess this document's relative importance—to the author and to the organization. Ask the writer what help is needed.

Be tactful. No one likes to feel criticized. If possible, read the document out of the author's presence. Don't over-edit.

Read the entire document through to get a sense of its logic and style:

- What is the point?

- What is the sequence of ideas? Look for gaps in reasoning and missing information.

- Consider the writer's point of view. Is there something you know that the writer needs to know?

- Identify the strengths and well-written parts.

- If you see errors in punctuation, spelling, or grammar, can they be categorized and described globally?

If you can, discuss this initial reaction with the author before making any written comments. Often, the help that is needed is with organization, and this can best be done in discussion—before the actual editing. In this conversation, listen for any additional points the author mentions that should be included. Reserve minor details for later. The author may want to revise the document before you comment further.

▶ Editing on the Document Itself

Avoid the schoolteacher stance!

Begin with as much praise as possible. Give a general comment
that covers the good parts first and then address what needs to
be changed.

Make as few marks as possible on the words. Phrase your
comments as questions whenever you can. For electronic
documents, use markups in your word-processing program.
For paper documents, write comments in the margin.
Underline or highlight a passage that you recommend be
revised. If corrections are necessary, use a colored pen (not
black) to make neat, small changes that are easy to see.

Suggest alternate phrasing where possible. The author may be
unaware of a better way to present an idea.

Refer the writer to sections of this book that will be helpful.
Give appropriate page numbers to save the author time.

36 WRITING FOR OTHERS

When you are asked to write material (a letter or speech) that someone else will sign or present, be very clear about what you have been asked to do.

▶ CLARIFYING THE REQUEST

Before you leave your colleague's office, be sure you know the answers to the following questions:

Freedom Have you been given freedom to write this however you wish, or will you need to get approval?

Information What help or information will you need?

Deadline Have you been given a realistic deadline? If you see a time crunch ahead, tell your colleague immediately.

Purpose Is the document or presentation intended to be persuasive or informative?

Audience Who will read (or hear) it? The audience will determine the tone. Ask for guidance if you're unsure.

Length and format Is the expected length rough or exact? Is there a model for the format desired?

▶ WRITING A SPEECH FOR ANOTHER

When writing a speech for someone else to deliver, strive for an easy delivery, with a tone appropriate to the content—preferably in the style of the speaker.

Read it aloud.

- Simplify places where you stumble; change parts where you find yourself rephrasing.

- Build in pauses for dramatic delivery.

- Be sure, above all, that it is absolutely correct—both in content and mechanics.

PART

FIVE

CORRECTNESS— USAGE

▶ A WORD ABOUT CORRECTNESS

Too much concern about correctness can inhibit your writing, so defer the fear of errors until you have your first draft. On the other hand, recognize that basic errors in writing can cost you prestige, time—and even money. We encourage you to master the few rules presented here as quickly as possible so that you can feel secure about your writing. Once that happens, you'll be free to concentrate on what you want to say.

37 COMMONLY CONFUSED WORDS

Spell checkers won't help you when you correctly spell the wrong word.

a, an, the	Use *a* before words starting with consonant sounds or long *u* (*a bat, a coat, a union*).
	Use *an* before words starting with vowels or pronounced as if they did (*an age, an egg, an hour, an M&M*).
	Use *the* rather than *a* or *an* when referring to one specific item.
	Please use the designated car service when traveling for this account.
	Use *a* or *an* rather than *the* when referring to any one out of a group.
	The client will pay for a car and driver at each end of your trip.
accept	To take, to receive
	This office does not accept collect phone calls.
except	Not including
	Laundry products—except for ours—leave an invisible film that attracts dirt.
affect	To change or influence
	Casual encounters in the office can affect morale.
effect	The result, the consequence
	Effect is usually a noun, so you'll find *the* or *an* in front.
	Social scientists have studied the effects of noise levels on productivity in the workplace.
allusion	Reference, what was alluded to
	Kiki's allusion to last year's private negotiations was inappropriate.

delusion	Fantasy
	He is under the delusion that the vice president is his buddy.
elision	Omission
	Your elision—whether by computer error or neglect—cost us the contract.
illusion	Dream, artificial image
	The projector creates an illusion of snow falling.

---

amount, number	Use *amount* for substances that cannot be counted (an amount of water).
	Use *number* for items that can be counted (a number of water bottles).

---

as far as . . . goes, as for/ regarding	*As far as* begins an expression that is incomplete without a verb—such as *goes* or *is concerned*—followed by an explanation. When writing, it is preferable to use *regarding* or *as for*.
	As far as the investors are concerned, they are enthusiastic.
	As for the investors, they are enthusiastic.

---

bare	Exposed, to uncover
	Protect your bare back with sunscreen.
	Please bare your wrist so we can measure it for the watchband.
bear	The animal; to carry (past tense, *bore*; past participle, *borne*)
	I do not intend to bear the responsibility for this project single-handedly.
	Scott bore up well during that brutal press conference.
	Prior to this pregnancy, the patient has borne four children without complications.

brake	The mechanism that stops the engine; to halt any motion
	Let's put the brakes on this spending trend.
	Brake on the approach; accelerate on the curve.
break	A separation; to shatter or separate into pieces or parts
	After the break, we will resume the negotiations.
	Let's break for dinner.
	Don't break the seal if you plan to return the software.

---

choose	Present tense (rhymes with *news*)
	Frank Gehry chooses pliable materials for his architecture.
chose	Past tense (rhymes with *nose*)
	We chose the applicant who had some maturity.

---

conscience	The sense of right and wrong
	Mr. Bradstreet claims to have a clear conscience regarding the distribution of bonuses.
conscious	Aware
	We became conscious of the need to widen our market.

---

desert	Arid country (accent on the first syllable); to abandon (accent on the second syllable)
deserts	What one deserved—good or bad; always plural (accent on the second syllable)
	After three days in the desert, the cinematographer deserted the project. That is just deserts for the ad executive who decided to schedule the shoot in August.
dessert	The sweet portion of the meal (accent on the second syllable)
	We will feature an article on frozen desserts.

etc., and so forth	*Etc.* is the abbreviation of *et cetera* (Latin for "and so forth"). "And so forth" is preferable. However, don't use "and etc."—which means "and and so forth."
	For a nominal fee, we can personalize the paper goods for your office party (table runners, napkins, beverage containers, etc.).

---

fewer, less	Use *fewer* for items that can be counted (fewer problems).
	Use *less* for substances or intangibles that cannot be counted (less dissatisfaction).

---

flower	Blossom, to flourish
	The children's art program is flowering in surprising ways.
flour	Ground grain or nuts
	Use semolina flour for making pasta.

---

good, well	*Well* can refer to one's health (an adjective) or to the way one performs (an adverb). *Good* is always an adjective, referring to having better quality.
	Barbara Withers supervises well.
	Ms. Withers is a good supervisor.
	But note these tricky cases:
	Olivia looks good. (She's good-looking.)
	Rivka looks well. (She no longer looks sick.)
	Clara sees well. (Her eyes work.)

---

hoard	To store
horde	Large, often unruly group
	The script requires the old woman to hoard her jewelbox in the cave as the hordes of soldiers cross the river.

it's	*It is.* Test by substituting "it is."
	It's finished. It's time to go.
its	Possessive
	Every goat is attached to its own legs.
	The pharmacy closed its doors December 1st.
	[No apostrophe. *It is* cannot be substituted.]

---

lay	To put something down
	-ing: Tim is laying the report in the chairman's hands at this very moment.
	Past tense: *laid*
	Tim laid the report on the chairman's desk early this morning.
	Once you *lay* something down, it *lies* there.
lie	To recline, to stay down; also, to tell a lie
	The new binding will allow the opened book to lie flat.
	Past tense (here's the tricky part): *lay*
	The report lay unnoticed under the tea tray.
	[*Lied* always means "told a lie."]
lying	Reclining
	I'd recommend lying low till the directors meet.
	Telling a lie
	Unfortunately, our supplier was lying about the delivery date.

---

lead	A metal (rhymes with *red*); to provide direction (rhymes with *reed*)
	Place a lead apron over the patient's body during dental X rays.
	Mr. Casey leads the sales force—surpassing his quota each quarter.

led	Past tense of *lead*
	Ms. Salina led the department in this year's fund raiser.
loose	Not tight (rhymes with *goose*)
	After Helene dieted for two weeks, her shoes and rings were loose.
lose	To misplace (rhymes with *news*)
	Please call this number if you lose your password.
	To be defeated
	I win; you lose.
of, have	Could have, should have, would have—not would of
passed	An exam, a car, a football; also passed away (died)
	This moisturizer has passed the most stringent dermatological tests.
past	Yesterdays (the past; past events); also, beyond
	Our past accomplishments are good predictors of success.
	Those policies were corrected in the past.
	Our office is two miles past the railroad tracks.
pore	Opening in covering or skin; to study carefully
	Minuscule pores in this fabric provide comfort during exercise.
	I expect you to pore over every aspect of the report before Monday.
pour	To transfer out by tipping the container; heavy rainfall
	We've been pouring funds into this project with no visible results.

quiet	Spike Jones rarely played quiet music.
quit	The lighting designer did not quit work until 2 a.m.
quite	Hippos are quite fast, considering their bulk.

---

so, very so . . . that	Avoid using *so* when you mean *very*. Instead of "Their hammock is so strong," write "Their hammock is very strong," or better yet, "Their hammock survived all the strength and durability tests." It is correct to use *so* when it is followed by *that*: "Their hammock is so strong that a 300-pound man can use it."

---

sole	Solitary, the only one; a fish
soul	Spirit; soul food, soul music
	Catfish, not sole, is better for this soul food recipe.
	The sole survivor of the riot remains in a coma.

---

than	Comparison
	Mr. Hacz is more skillful with facts and figures than with people.
then	Next
	Make certain that the primary coat is thoroughly dry; then apply the first coat of color.

---

their	Something is theirs. (One way to remember: Heirs own things.)
	The employees rate their flexible hours as the primary benefit.
there	A place: Go over there. (All the place words end in -*ere*.)
	There is . . . There are . . . There was . . . There were
	There are several alternatives to Ms. Verona's offer.
they're	They are.
	They're trying hard to be polite.

to	Direction
	Give it to me.
	Go to New York.
	A verb form
	To see, to run, to be
	(Note that you barely pronounce *to*.)
too	More than enough
	Too hot, too bad, too late, too much
	Also
	Me, too!
	(Note that you pronounce *too* clearly.)
two	2

_____

ware	Utility items, gear
	Vacuum cleaner salespeople used to sell their wares door to door.
	Some hardware stores now sell software and underwear as well.
wear	What one puts on one's body; what happens with use
	Wear different shoes on alternate days to avoid wearing them out too soon.
were	Past tense
	You were, we were, they were
we're	We are
	We're a nation of immigrants.
where	A place
	Where are the prototypes now?

_____

weather	Rain or snow
whether	If
	Please let me know whether you can meet the new deadline.

who's	Who is
	Who's there?
	Who's coming with us?
whose	Possessive
	Whose diamond is this?

---

woman	One person
	Hannah Productions hired a woman for the job.
	a woman; a man
women	Several of them
	More and more women fly their own planes.

---

worse	When comparing *two* things, one is *worse* than the other.
worst	When comparing *three or more* things, one is *the worst*. *The* almost always comes before *worst*.

---

your	Belonging to you. Use only for *your* mail, *your* job, and so on.
	I did not receive your message yesterday.
	Your cannot be used when you mean "you are."
you're	You are
	I'd like to know what you're thinking.

38 ONE WORD OR TWO?

If you can put another word between, keep them separate. Otherwise, check this list.

---

all ready	The storyboards are all ready for the presentation.
	They are all completely ready.
already	The agents have already taken their percentage.

---

all right	(always two words)
	It's all right with the client to schedule delivery for next week.
	(*Alright* is not an acceptable spelling.)

---

a long	The last confrontation required a long time to resolve.
along	Our journey will take us along the Natchez Trace.

---

a lot	(always two words)
	We owe you a lot—a whole lot.
	(*A lot* is not to be confused with *allot*—meaning "to allocate.")

---

a part	We found that Ms. Velasquez was a part of every project—a significant part.
apart	Unplug the fan before you take it apart for cleaning.

---

at least	(always two words)
	You'll need at least three disks to back up this program.

each other	(always two words)
	When assigning team members, consider how they've worked with each other before.

---

even though	(always two words)
	She will run again for office even though she has never won an election.

---

everybody	Jimmy's comments incensed everybody in the chat room.
	But: Every body was given a decent burial.

---

every day	It rains every day, every single day.
everyday	There is a difference between dress-down and everyday clothes.

---

every one	Every one of the associates will be eligible for the bonus.
everyone	Everyone likes pizza.

---

in fact	(always two words)
	In fact, the real truth never came out.
in order	(always two words)
	I paid the bill ahead of time in order to avoid confusion.
in spite of	(always three words)
	We exceeded our sales quotas in spite of a reduction in personnel.
intact	I recommend that we keep the mailroom team intact.
into	Pour the batter into the heated and buttered popover pan.

in touch	(always two words)
	Stay in touch via email.

itself	(always one word)
	The snake wrapped itself around the boy's arm.
myself	I promised myself that we'd never ask such sacrifices of our people again.
	But: My self-esteem was at stake.

nobody	Nobody knows how Rebecca Fraser manages to juggle so many problems so cheerfully and so successfully.
	But: No body in the temporary morgue has been identified.
no one	No one on the current staff speaks Spanish.

nowadays	(always one word)
	Nowadays, you don't hear the word "icebox."
nevertheless	(always one word)
	Nevertheless, we expect the merger to be approved.
somehow	(always one word)
	The package was somehow shipped to Mississippi instead of Minnesota.

some time	We'll reconvene some time next month.
sometimes	Sometimes, I wonder why I continue to work.

throughout	(always one word)
	The research assistant was kept busy throughout the entire summer.

whenever   (always one word)

                 The mood lightens whenever that CD is played.

whereas   (always one word)

                 We can change colors at little expense, whereas
                 costs for changes in lighting will be prohibitive.

wherever   (always one word)

                 People flock to him wherever he goes.

———————————

withhold   (always one word)

                 Until the roof has been repaired, we will withhold
                 the rent.

without   (always one word)

                 Several days passed without a glimmer of sunlight.

39 SPELLING

There's no getting around it. Correct spelling of words in English takes patience. However, you can save time by learning the rules—particularly for those words a spellchecker won't catch.

▶ *I* BEFORE *E*

Use *I* before *E*
Except after *C*
Or when sounded like *A*
As in *neighbor* and *weigh*.

believe	deceive	freight
friend	receive	vein
piece	conceit	

Exceptions:

weird	foreign	leisure	seize	their

▶ WORD ENDINGS

The quiet *-ed* endings

Three *-ed* endings are not always pronounced clearly, but they need to be written.

used to   supposed to   prejudiced

-sk and *-st* endings

When *s* is added to words like these, it isn't always clearly pronounced, but it still needs to be there.

asks	consists	psychologists
risks	insists	scientists
desks	suggests	terrorists
tasks	costs	interests

The -y endings

- When a verb ends in *y*, keep the *y* when you add *ing*. To add *s* or *ed*, change the *y* to *i*.

crying	cries	cried
studying	studies	studied
trying	tries	tried

- When a noun ends in *y*, make it plural by changing the *y* to *i* and adding *es*.

activities	families	theories

Exception: Simply add *s* to nouns ending in *ey*.

attorneys	monkeys	valleys

p or *pp*? *t* or *tt*?

Listen to the vowel before the added part.

- If the vowel is long (sounds like its own letter name), use only one consonant:

writer	writing

The *i* in *writer* sounds like the name of the letter *i*, so use only one *t*.

- If the vowel before the added part is short (has a different sound from its name), double the consonant:

written

The *i* sounds like the *i* in *it*, so you double the *t*.

The same method works for *hoping* and *hopping*. Listen for the different sounds of the letter *o*.

Here are some other examples:

beginning	dropping	quitting
stopped	occurred	referred

An exception: *coming*

► WORDS WITH PREFIXES AND SUFFIXES

When you add a prefix or suffix, you usually keep the spelling of the root word.

misspell	suddenness	dissatisfaction
hopeful	disappear	government
unnoticed	environment	

The -*ly* endings also follow this rule. Do not drop a letter when you add -*ly*.

really   totally   lonely   finally   unfortunately

But *truly* does not follow the rule.

Exception: The final *e* is usually dropped before a suffix that starts with a vowel.

debatable   sensible   lovable

► TRICKY WORDS

Look hard at the middle of each word:

de**finite**ly	em**bar**rass	usu**al**ly
se**par**ate	ac**com**modate	ne**ces**sary
re**pet**ition	pro**bab**ly	famil**i**ar
o**pin**ion	int**er**est	

40 CAPITALIZATION

Capitalize names of people, organizations, localities, days of the week, and months. Do not capitalize for emphasis.

▶ DO CAPITALIZE

- Names or initials of people, companies, departments, and organizations

    Tenants and Neighbors Coalition

    B. B. Thornton

    FDA (Federal Drug Administration)

- Business or family names like *Group, Agency, Firm, Mother,* or *Grandfather* only when used as a name or with a name

    I will be happy to meet with a representative from your firm Tuesday morning.

    This is the biscuit recipe Aunt Adelaide would have used sixty years ago.

    Please forward your résumé to the Human Resources Department.

- People's titles when they precede their names

    Dr. Judd   Vice President Jan Peters   Major Gross

- Days of the week, months of the year

    Wednesday   February

- Brand names

    Kleenex   Coca-Cola   Domino's Pizza

    (But not the product itself if it is not part of the company's name—thus, *Crest toothpaste*.)

- Public holidays

    Thanksgiving   Fourth of July

143

- The entire name of a specific place, event, and so on

     Oak Street   Battle of Gettysburg   Calhoun High School

- In titles, the first word, major words, and words of five letters or more

     Die Broke   "A Rose for Emily"

     Around the World in Eighty Days   *All Things Considered*

     "If the Devil Danced in Empty Pockets, He'd Have a Ball in Mine"

▶ DO NOT CAPITALIZE

- Words for business or relationships like *firm, committee, department, boss, sister* after *the, a, my, his, her, their, our, your*

     our department head   your firm   her brother

     the real estate business   the organization

     My agency hopes to hire three programmers this month.

- Titles of people separate from their names, unless the title is used in lieu of a (perhaps unknown) name.

     We will hire a new marketing vice president in January.

     The Vice President for Human Resources must attend every negotiating session.

- Seasons of the year

     spring   autumn

- Generic names

     facial tissues   soda pop   pizza

- Private celebrations

     birthday   anniversary

- A type of place, event, and so on

     a dark street   the eve of battle   high school

- Most diseases

     diabetes   cancer   tuberculosis

But note: Alzheimer's disease (the discoverer's name is capitalized) and AIDS.

- For emphasis

    Do not capitalize whole words (AMNESIA); do not capitalize an entire agenda or Internet message.

41 ABBREVIATIONS AND NUMBERS

Abbreviations and numbers must be clear and easily read.

▶ ABBREVIATIONS

As a general rule, don't use abbreviations in formal documents. Abbreviate freely in informal messages—as long as the abbreviation is unambiguous.

FORMAL DOCUMENTS

Avoid abbreviating words within your sentences when writing formally. Particularly avoid such abbreviations as these:

Dept.   VP   thru   Co.

Do abbreviate the company name or repeated technical terms after fully spelling them out first. Do not use periods after such abbreviations.

> Widget Productions Incorporated has always been proud of quality control, so we are doubly embarrassed about your defective corkscrew. In addition to a replacement, WPI is pleased to send you two decorative wine stoppers.

Always abbreviate common titles with proper names:

Mr. Smithers   Ms. Pendergrast   St. Bartholomew

Abbreviate *doctor* only before a name:

the doctor   Dr. Salk

Do not abbreviate most other titles—whether preceding or following the name:

Vice President Witherspoon

Margery Jamieson, Associate Editor

INFORMAL DOCUMENTS

In informal communications (such as email and in-house notes to colleagues), conventional abbreviations, including technical terms used in your industry, are acceptable, even preferable.

> The meeting with all DAs is scheduled for 10 a.m., Thurs., Apr. 21.

Avoid abbreviating a word that might be misinterpreted.

> Please discuss the rev. with James. (review? revision?)

▶ NUMBERS

SPELL OUT

- Numbers that take only one or two words

  > nine   twenty-seven   two billion

- Numbers that begin a sentence

  > One hundred four years ago the ship sank.
  >
  > The ship sank 104 years ago.

- Numbers that form a compound word

  > a two-year-old baby

- Fractions

  > one-half

USE NUMERALS FOR

- Numbers that require three or more words

  > 1,889   162

- Dates, exact times, page references, room numbers, statistics, addresses, percentages, and dollars and cents

  > May 6, 1974   7,500 residents   99.44%
  >
  > page 2   221 B Baker Street   2:30 p.m.

- A list or series of numbers

  > 1, 4, 9, 16, 25
  >
  > seats 12, 14, and 16

42 CORRECT PRONOUNS

I, she, he, we, they, and *who* identify the persons doing the action. *Me, her, him, us, them,* and *whom* identify the persons receiving the action.

► PAIRS: MY PARTNER AND I/ MY PARTNER AND ME

- With a pair of people, try the sentence without the other person:

  Carter gave the account to my partner and me.
  (Carter gave the account to me, *not* to I.)

  The client had already sent my colleagues and me her deposit.
  (She sent . . . me her deposit, *not* she sent . . . I her deposit.)

  The same rule goes for *him, her, he, she.*

  The producer met with Carolyn and her.
  (The producer met with her, *not* with she.)

- Don't be afraid of *me*; it's often right.

  Between you and me, Kevin is in over his head.
  (*Not* Between you and I . . .)

  Don't use *myself* when *me* will do.

  I did the graphics myself.
  (Here, *me* cannot be substituted.)

  Sam did the graphics for Toby and me.
  (*Not* . . . for Toby and myself.)

► COMPARISONS

- Use *I, he, she, we, they* when comparing with the subject of the sentence—usually the first person in the sentence.

  Ms. Jason was less responsible for supervising Sarah than I was.

  Mr. Schultz is more easily distracted than she is.

  Sometimes *is* or *was* is left off the end:

  Mr. Schultz is more easily distracted than she.

- Use *me, him, her, us, them* when comparing with the receiver, the object of the sentence—usually the person mentioned later in the sentence.

   > The quality of the software is less important to John's team than to us.

   Note the difference:

   > The judge listened more carefully to Agnes than me.
   > (The judge listened more carefully to Agnes than to me.)

   > The judge listened more carefully to Agnes than I.
   > (The judge listened more carefully to Agnes than I did.)

▶ WHO/WHOM

- Use *whom* after prepositions (to whom, of whom, for whom, from whom, with whom).

   > To whom should I address my complaint?

- Use *who* for subjects of verbs.

   > Who should I say is calling?

   When you're in doubt, *who* is usually acceptable.

- Use *who* for people—not *which.*

   > The runner who finished last got all the publicity.

43 CONSISTENT PRONOUNS

Make a conscious choice of your pronouns. Don't shift from *a person* to *they* to *you* to *I*.

▶ THE SINGULAR/PLURAL PROBLEM: *THE CUSTOMER... THEIR*

In common speech, we often use *they* or *their* to refer back to a singular noun.

> The customer should get their money back, no questions asked.

> If a person wants to succeed in real estate, they should come to our seminar.

> Unless someone has a strong background in music, they won't understand this project.

The customer, a person, and *someone* are singular; *they* and *their* are plural. Although you will hear this usage in conversation and will even see it in print, it is still not acceptable in most writing.

If you keep the singular noun, you will need a singular pronoun. Here are your options.

He, he or she

The old-fashioned pronoun choice to accompany *a person* or *someone* is *he*:

> Unless someone has a strong background in music, he won't understand this project.

This choice, however, presumes that *a person* is male. It should be avoided because it is sexist language. *He or she* is possible, but not if it comes several times in a row; *he or she,* when repeated, becomes clunky and awkward. Avoid *he/she* and *s/he*.

> When a person is not afraid of criticism, he or she will not worry about what others think of him or her.

One

One means *a person*—singular.

> If one wants to succeed in real estate, one should come to our seminar.

The problem here is that *one* sounds stuffy in American English. How many times can one say *one* before one makes oneself sound silly?

FOUR SOLUTIONS

A real person

Often, your best choice is to use a true-to-life example, a real person:

> Marc Frontenac hoped to succeed in real estate; after taking our seminar, his business doubled.

A real example not only makes the grammar correct, but it is also much more interesting and memorable. *A person* and *someone* are nobodies.

Plural

Instead of *the customer,* use *customers;* instead of *a person* or *someone,* try *people,* which fits with *they.*

> The customers should get their money back, no questions asked.

> If people want to succeed in real estate, they should come to our seminar.

You

You is uncomplicated and inviting when you are generalizing.

> If you want to succeed in real estate, you should come to our seminar.

> If you don't have a background in music, you won't be able to understand this project.

No pronoun

Many times, you can avoid the problem entirely by recasting the sentence.

> The customer's money should be refunded, no questions asked.

▶ Slippery Pronouns: *You, I, We*

Writers often get tangled up in their pronouns when trying to avoid *I* or *you*. However, using *I* or *you* makes for strong writing— particularly in letters and memos.

You

Of course, *you* is best for directly addressing your reader or listener. The problem with *you* comes when you find yourself sliding back and forth between *you* and other pronouns.

> I have several concerns over Mr. Jerrold's performance. When a crisis arose, you suddenly could not locate him.

Here, the writer says *you*, but really means *I* and should say so:

> Whenever a crisis arose, I rarely could find him.

In any case, check for inconsistency and choose the best pronoun.

I

Don't be afraid of *I* if that's who you mean. In the right place, *I* has both warmth and the ring of truth.

> I am convinced that reducing staff now will hurt us in the long run.
>
> I have no hesitation in recommending Cynthia Jackson to you as an outstanding candidate for the position of advertising director.

We

We is appropriate when you are speaking for your company, your department, or your working group; it can also be used to mean people in general. *We* sometimes has more authority than just plain *I* and has the advantage of deflecting criticism or blame from any one person.

> We see no problem in continuing to use the incinerator we have now.

> We recommend a 10 percent increase in price immediately.

Be careful when you use *we* that you mean more than just yourself; using *I* might be more appropriate and honest.

44 PRONOUNS: AVOIDING VAGUENESS

Certain pronouns—*which, it, this,* and *that*—must refer to a single word, not to a whole phrase. Keep them near the word they refer to; eliminate them where you can.

These words are used loosely in conversation, but in most writing you should use them more precisely.

Which

Which causes the most trouble of the four. Often, it can be eliminated.

> *Imprecise:* Last month's sales offset the previous month's decline by 21 percent, which means projections for the year are holding.

> *Precise:* Last month's sales offset the previous month's decline by 21 percent; the net result means projections for the year are holding.

Use *in which* only when you mean that one thing is inside the other:

> The canisters in which we store nitrogen dioxide are leaking.

Which cannot start a sentence unless it asks a question.

It, this, or that

When you use *it*, make sure the reader knows what *it* is. When *this* or *that* seems unclear, add a noun, such as this *product* or that *outcome.*

> *Imprecise:* You need to bring the revised contracts, the presentation materials, and sixteen copies of your own report. It's urgent!

> *Precise:* We urgently need the revised contracts, the presentation materials, and sixteen copies of your own report.

Imprecise: The focus group preferred design No. 601 for the eye shadow containers; the lowest bid is for $250 per 100 count. This means we can proceed.

Precise: The focus group preferred design No. 601 for the eye shadow containers; the lowest bid is for $250 per 100 count. These positive results mean we can proceed.

Imprecise: We are not paid well and receive inadequate benefits, but I don't think that we can discuss that yet.

Precise: We are not paid well and receive inadequate benefits, but I don't think that we can discuss benefits yet.

45 VERBS: AGREEMENT WITH SUBJECTS

No matter how far apart they are, the subject and verb must agree. The word before the verb is not always its subject. Look for who or what is doing the action.

- Two singular subjects joined by *and* (for example, *the cologne* and *the aftershave*) make a plural and need a plural verb.

    The cologne and the aftershave complement each other.

    The morning shift coordinator and the afternoon maintenance supervisor have not agreed to the new schedule.

- Sometimes an insertion separates the subject and verb.

    The juice blend, not the other beverages, needs chilling.

    The lady who sells flowers has a mysterious voice.

- The subject cannot be the word that directly follows *of*; read the sentence without the prepositional phrase.

    One of the accountants was lenient on entertainment expenses.
    (*One* is the subject, not *accountants.*)

    Each of us accepts responsibility for the delay.

    The use of acupuncture needles has tripled.

- The subject of the sentence <u>follows</u> *there was, there were, there is, there are.*

    There is an embarrassing typo in the auto mechanics' manual.
    (*Typo* is the subject.)

    There were two causes for this power failure.
    (*Causes* is the subject.)

- Words with *one* and *body* are singular.

    Everyone agrees that the warranty was poorly written.

    Somebody always overheats the copying machine.

- Sometimes a group can be singular.

    My family does not eat crowder peas.

Our company provides dental insurance for its employees.

A thousand dollars is a lot of cash to carry around.

- *-ing* phrases are usually singular.

    Dating two people is tricky.

46 VERBS: CONSISTENT TENSES

Sometimes you may find yourself slipping back and forth between present and past verb tenses. Be consistent, especially within each paragraph.

▶ PRESENT TENSE AND PAST TENSE

- Use the present tense for describing actions that continue to happen regularly.

  > Ms. Chu is responsible for our San Francisco region.

  > Val Codresciu designs all our brochures.

- Use the simple past tense to tell your own stories or stories from history.

  > The first time I tried Jello I was four years old.

  > President Truman waved from the caboose.

▶ TROUBLESOME VERBS

HAD

Watch out for *had:* You often don't need it. Use *had* to refer to events that were already finished when your story or example took place—the past before the past that you're describing. To check, try adding *previously* or *already* next to *had*.

  > In 1986, the firm moved to New York. We had practiced in Florida for three years.

  > If I had known about tse-tse flies, I would have been much more cautious.

WOULD

Most of the time, you can leave out *would*. Use it for something that happened regularly during a period of the past.

  > In the early days of automobiles, tires would blow out routinely.

Also use *would* for hypothetical situations.

> I would have preferred hiring Spencer.
>
> If we had hired Spencer, we would have that account in Japan right now.
>
> If Grayson were more responsible, we would never have lost that account.

(Use *were* with a singular subject after *if* or *as though*.)

COULD, CAN

- Use *could* to refer to the past and *can* to refer to the present.

> *Past:* The engineers couldn't run the experiment because the ocean was too rough.
>
> *Present:* The engineers can't run the experiment because the ocean is too rough.

- Use *could* to show what might happen and doesn't; use *can* to show ability.

> This company makes huge profits. It could provide free day care. (It doesn't.)
>
> This company makes such huge profits that it can provide free day care. (It does.)

47 WORD ENDINGS: S AND *ED*

If word endings give you problems, train yourself to check every noun to see if it needs *s* and every verb to see if it needs *s* or *ed*. Note that often these endings are barely pronounced.

ADD *ED*

- To form most simple past tenses

    She walked.   He tripped.   Mae asked a question.

- After *has, have, had*

    He has walked.   We have moved.   She had already arrived.

- After the *be* verbs (*are, were, is, was, am, be, been, being*)

    This manager was prejudiced against immigrants.

    That real estate market is depressed.

    Marge Zolanski is engaged to be married.

Note that the *-ed* ending can sometimes appear in present and future tenses:

    The gifts for premium customers are supposed to arrive on Friday.

    Following his speech, Mr. Poppins will be prepared to respond to reporters' questions.

DO NOT ADD *ED*

- After *to*

    Rosa Sanchez preferred to work with our most difficult cases.

- After *would, should, could*

    Sometimes she would work on weekends.

    This patient should walk for an hour every day.

- After *did, didn't*

    This software didn't save us any time.

160

- After an irregular past tense

    We bought the new system.

    The stock fell.

    The shoes cost only seventeen dollars.

ADD *S*

- To form a plural (more than one)

    many scientists   two potatoes

- To the present tense of a verb that follows *he, she, it,* or a singular noun

    He reports to the two vice presidents.

    She asks provocative questions.

    Polly insists on using the latest version.

    It costs very little.

Note: Usually when there is an *s* on the noun, there is no *s* on the verb.

    Pots rattle.

    A pot rattles.

    The candles burn swiftly.

    The candle burns swiftly.

- To form a possessive (with an apostrophe)

    the director's requirements

    today's society

    Ms. Salama's office

    women's clothing

DO NOT ADD *S* TO A VERB

- If the subject of the sentence is plural or if there are two subjects

    Tulips come from Holland.

    Salt and sugar look the same.

- If one of these helping verbs comes before the main verb

| does | may | will | shall | can |
| must | might | would | should | could |

  Mr. Smoot can clear up all your software conflicts.

  A heavy rainstorm might ruin this carefully planned reception.

  The new regulation does make me angry.

For more help with word endings, see Chapters 39, 45, 46, and 53 ("Spelling," "Verbs: Agreement with Subjects," "Verbs: Consistent Tenses," and "Apostrophes").

PART
SIX

CORRECTNESS—
PUNCTUATION

48 PERIODS: AVOIDING SENTENCE FRAGMENTS AND RUN-ON SENTENCES

Often you reach a pause in your writing, and you wonder, "Do I put a comma or a period?" The length of a sentence has nothing to do with the right choice. You need to look at what comes before and after the punctuation to see whether you have two separate sentences or a sentence plus a sentence fragment.

▶ RECOGNIZING SENTENCE FRAGMENTS

WORDS THAT RARELY BEGIN SENTENCES

Certain words almost never begin sentences:

such as	when	
especially	which	
that	who	except in a question
not	how	
like, just like	what	
the same as		

These words extend the previous sentence. In most cases, put a comma or a dash before these words.

Incorrect: The attached report was translated from the Japanese original. Which was based on Monday morning's data.

Correct: The attached report was translated from the Japanese original, which was based on Monday morning's data.

Incorrect: Since 1977, Michael Kahn has edited all of Steven Spielberg's films. Such as *Close Encounters of the Third Kind* and *Saving Private Ryan*.

> *Correct:* Since 1977, Michael Kahn has edited all of Steven Spielberg's films—such as *Close Encounters of the Third Kind* and *Saving Private Ryan.*

> *Incorrect:* I believe that Whitman is our most successful salesperson. That he single-handedly built up American Pottery.

> *Correct:* I believe that Whitman is our most successful salesperson, that he single-handedly built up American Pottery.

Note: *That* rarely begins a sentence, except when it points, as in "That was the year of the great flood."

SUBORDINATING WORDS

Certain words always begin half a sentence—either the first half or the second half. These are called *subordinating words.*

when	if
before	because
after	although (even though)
as	unless
while	since

A sentence fragment often begins with a subordinating word:

> *Incorrect:* Even though I always fly business class.

You can fix this fragment by connecting it to the sentence before or after it:

> *Correct:* I find air travel extremely stressful even though I always fly business class.

> *Correct:* Even though I always fly business class, I find air travel extremely stressful.

You can also drop the subordinating word:

> *Correct:* I find air travel extremely stressful.

A subtle point: Watch out for *and*. Putting *and* between a fragment and a sentence doesn't fix the fragment:

> *Still incorrect:* Even though I always fly business class and I find air travel extremely stressful.

VERB FORMS THAT CREATE FRAGMENTS

Certain verb forms cannot be the only verb in the sentence.

Verbs Ending in *-ing*

> *Incorrect:*   This film abounds with irreverent energy. Carrying the audience along with outrageous humor.

One solution is to connect the fragment to the previous sentence:

> *Correct:*   This film abounds with irreverent energy, carrying the audience along with outrageous humor.

The second solution is to change the *-ing* verb to a complete verb:

> *Correct:*   This film abounds with irreverent energy. It carries the audience along with outrageous humor.

An *-ing* verb can begin a sentence if a complete verb comes later:

> *Correct:*   Keeping the audience in hysterics is Mel Brooks's trademark.

To Verbs (Infinitives)

To verbs also frequently begin fragments:

> *Incorrect:*   Here's a voucher for two tickets to *The Lion King* with our compliments. To apologize for inconveniencing you this morning.

Fix these fragments by connecting them to the sentence before or by adding a subject and verb:

> *Correct:*   Here's a voucher for two tickets to *The Lion King* with our compliments, to apologize for inconveniencing you this morning.

Correct: Here's a voucher for two tickets to *The Lion King* with our compliments. We wish to apologize for inconveniencing you this morning.

REPEATED WORDS

A repeated word can begin a fragment:

Incorrect: Elizabeth is the ideal supervisor. A supervisor who is both encouraging and demanding.

The best solution here is to replace the period with a comma.

Correct: Elizabeth is the ideal supervisor, a supervisor who is both encouraging and demanding.

▶ HOW TO FIX FRAGMENTS

- Attach the fragment to the previous sentence.

    Incorrect: Of course talking to your plants helps them grow. Because you're giving them a good dose of carbon dioxide.

    Correct: Of course talking to your plants helps them grow because you're giving them a good dose of carbon dioxide.

- Change the phrasing or omit the word that points to the previous sentence. Often this word will be a subordinating word.

    Correct: Of course talking to your plants helps them grow. You're giving them a good dose of carbon dioxide.

- Change the verb or add a verb (and, if necessary, a subject).

    Incorrect: I'm writing to commend Tony Zurlo to your attention. To provide further evidence of his considerable expertise.

    Correct: I'm writing to commend Tony Zurlo to your attention. I hope to provide further evidence of his considerable expertise.

USING FRAGMENTS FOR STYLE

Professional writers use sentence fragments for emphasis or style. Once you have control over the basics of sentence structure and punctuation, you can experiment. In the right spot, fragments can be strong. Very strong.

▶ RECOGNIZING RUN-ON SENTENCES

A run-on sentence happens when you have two complete sentences, but you have only a comma or no punctuation between them. Run-ons usually occur because the two sentences are closely related. The two most common spots where run-ons occur are

- When a pronoun begins the second sentence:

  Incorrect: The news team has been stranded by the flood, they won't be able to deliver the tapes.

  Correct: The news team has been stranded by the flood. They won't be able to deliver the tapes.

  Incorrect: This lemon zester is ergonometrically designed, it's comfortable to use.

  Correct: This lemon zester is ergonometrically designed; it's comfortable to use.

- When *however* begins the second sentence:

  Incorrect: We can control the noise level in all the cubicles, however we will have to charge an additional fee.

  Correct: We can control the noise level in all the cubicles. However, we will have to charge an additional fee.

▶ HOW TO FIX RUN-ON SENTENCES

  Run-on: Our cleaning staff will keep your home ready for company, we're both thorough and fast.

- Insert a period between the two sentences.

> *Correct:* Our cleaning staff will keep your home ready for company. We're both thorough and fast.

- Insert a semicolon between the two sentences.

> *Correct:* Our cleaning staff will keep your home ready for company; we're both thorough and fast.

- Insert a comma and a coordinating conjunction between the two sentences.

> *Correct:* Our cleaning staff will keep your home ready for company, for we're both thorough and fast.

- Insert a subordinating word before one of the sentences.

> *Correct:* Our cleaning staff will keep your home ready for company because we're both thorough and fast.

► USING *BUT, HOWEVER, ALTHOUGH*

Notice the punctuation in these sentences:

> These three words are used to reverse the meaning of a sentence, but they are punctuated differently.

> These three words are used to reverse the meaning of a sentence; however, they are punctuated differently.

> These three words are used to reverse the meaning of a sentence although they are punctuated differently.

For an illustration of sentence structure, see "Anatomy of a Sentence" in the appendix of this book.

COMMAS

These days, more errors come from having too many commas than from having too few.

Writing trends, especially in business writing, have moved more and more into "open" punctuation—that is, punctuation which de-emphasizes the use of commas when a sentence can be clearly read without them. However, many businesses still adhere to "closed" punctuation—strict adherence to formal grammatical rules. When you elect to omit a comma, be certain that you are doing so as a choice, rather than as neglect.

Here are four places where commas are necessary.

▶ COMMA BEFORE
but and so yet or for nor

Put a comma before *but, and, so, yet, or, for,* and *nor* when they connect two sentences.

> The lead actor hobbled in on crutches, but the show went on.
>
> Rosette plays a hard game of tennis three times a week, and she intends to enter the county tournament next spring.
>
> Not only will a deskside paper shredder keep your desktop clear, but it will also ensure privacy of information.
>
> The agent took too long to respond, so we have withdrawn the offer.

However, don't automatically stick in a comma just because a sentence is long.

> Conferees are invited to meet for refreshments in the lobby at 6:45 p.m.

▶ COMMAS IN A LIST OR SERIES

Use commas between parts of a series of three or more.

In less than one month the game farm has saved the lives of a red fox, a great horned owl, a mountain lion, and a black bear cub.

The auctioneer moved through the hundred items rapidly, sold all but four of them, and kept the audience laughing the whole time.

Refinement   The final comma in a series (which usually precedes *and*) is sometimes omitted when not essential to the sense of the sentence.

The auctioneer moved through the hundred items rapidly, sold all but four of them and kept the audience laughing the whole time.

I wanted to buy toothpaste, jumper cables, a potted plant, cookies and fabric all in one store.

Take care, however, when omitting the final comma: be certain you don't need it for clarity.

In the waiting room sat a bearded man, a police officer, a woman eating a sandwich, and a parakeet in a cage.

(Without the last comma, what happens to the parakeet?)

Don't use a comma in a pair.

Rosette plays a hard game of tennis three times a week and intends to enter the county tournament next spring.

In one month the game farm saved the lives of a red fox and a great horned owl.

Sue and Brian volunteered to prepare the agenda and get the report to the subcommittee by Wednesday.

▶ Comma After a Lead-in

Use a comma after an introductory part of a sentence.

However, Ms. Capone has improved her presentation skills dramatically.

For example, state law requires an inventory of properties before the will can be probated.

Arthur, will you please keep notes on the proceedings?

After lunch, there will be a hands-on workshop in C319.

During the entire four hours of the hearing, the district attorney never even sat down.

When the Tokyo market closes on Friday, we will make another evaluation.

Refinement The comma is often omitted after a very short introductory word or phrase when you do not need or want a voice pause. Words such as *nevertheless, however,* and *therefore* generally take a comma because they require a voice pause. In the following examples, either sentence is considered correct.

After lunch, there will be a hands-on workshop in C319.
After lunch there will be a hands-on workshop in C319.

In time, we will all know exactly what happened.
In time we will all know exactly what happened.

▶ A PAIR OF COMMAS AROUND AN INSERTION

Surround an insertion or interruption with a pair of commas. Both commas are necessary, since a single comma would separate the subject from its verb.

The truth, however, finally came out.

Woody Guthrie, the father of Arlo Guthrie, wrote "This Land Is Your Land."

The office manager, Jennie Pocock, who leaves after twenty-two years of incomparable service, will be difficult to replace.

Judith Appelbaum, in her book *How to Get Happily Published,* gives numerous suggestions for working with a publisher or for going the self-publishing route.

Places and dates are treated as insertions. Note especially that commas surround the year and the state.

> Honesdale, Pennsylvania, was named for Philip Hone, former mayor of New York City and president of the coal company.

> I was born on August 15, 1954, at seven in the morning.

> Filming will begin in Sullivan Bay, British Columbia, March or April, 2005, depending on Ms. Wright's availability.

Refinement Commas are not used when the interruption is essential to the meaning of the sentence—that is, when the word or phrase could not be omitted.

> The scanner on the third floor is best for your project.
> (There are other scanners—on different floors.)

50 SEMICOLONS AND COLONS

Semicolons can be used instead of periods; they also can separate parts of a complicated list. Colons create suspense: they can set up a list, a quotation, or an emphatic statement.

► SEMICOLONS

Use a semicolon to connect two related sentences; each half must be a complete sentence.

> This company was in crisis two years ago; Jane Morgan's quiet professionalism made the transition to solvency possible.

> It's not that O'Hara's position is wrong; it's that he misses the key point.

A semicolon often comes before certain transition words; a comma follows the transition.

however	therefore	otherwise
nevertheless	in other words	instead
for example	on the other hand	meanwhile
besides	furthermore	fortunately

> Our competitors offer some important benefits; however, we offer those same benefits plus more, at a lower cost.

> The bank lost two of my deposits; therefore, I am closing my account.

Semicolons work best when used to emphasize a strong connection between the two sentences.

Use semicolons, instead of commas, in a list when some of the parts already have commas.

> To make it as an actor, you need, first of all, some natural talent; second, the habits of discipline and concentration; and third, the ability to promote yourself.

► COLONS

Use a colon after a complete sentence to introduce related details.

Before a colon you must have a complete statement. Don't use a colon after *are* or *include* or *such as.*

Colons can introduce

- A list

    In addition to bringing their personal supplies, clients are responsible for providing these items: a sleeping bag, a water bottle, and a backpack.

- A quotation

    The author begins with a shocker: "Mother spent her summer sitting naked on a rock."

- An example

    Increase your use of legumes: for example, beans or lentils.

- An emphatic assertion

    This is the bottom line: Meredith will reject the contract without a guarantee of protection for her heirs.

- A subtitle

    Rules of Thumb: A Guide for Writers

When you type, leave one space after a colon.

51 DASHES AND PARENTHESES

In general, dashes highlight or emphasize material, whereas parentheses de-emphasize the material within them.

DASHES

Dashes highlight the part of the sentence they separate, or show an abrupt change of thought in midsentence, or connect a fragment to a sentence.

> Artemesia—which craves dry heat—is the perfect border plant for rock gardens in the Southwest.
>
> Cell-phone conversations—or email messages, for that matter—should not be considered private.
>
> Johnson and Ryman will offer a substantial collection of Fiestaware—a collection remarkable for its pristine condition and variety of colors.

Dashes can replace a period, comma, colon, or semicolon. However—handy though they are—too many can make it seem as if you've dashed off your report.

When you type, use two hyphens or a one-em dash; there is no space before or after the dash.

PARENTHESES

Parentheses de-emphasize the words they separate. Use them to enclose brief explanations or interruptions. They can contain either part of a sentence or a whole sentence.

> We offered at the regional average price per acre ($995) and settled at $800.
>
> Ms. Hasie has had two extremely successful years in sales. (See the attached reports.)
>
> This proposal has plagued the creative team (three designers have worked on it without resolution); so at this point, I recommend that we decline the commission.

- Put any necessary punctuation after the second parenthesis if the parentheses contain part of a sentence.

- If the parentheses contain a complete sentence, put the period inside the second parenthesis. Notice, however, that you don't capitalize or use a period when parentheses enclose a sentence within a sentence.

Be sparing with parentheses. Too many can chop up your sentences.

52 HYPHENS

Hyphens join compound words.

- Compound words that are numbers, idioms, or created expressions require hyphens.

  seventy-five   in-laws   self-employed

  the getting-ready-for-a-first-date scene   slap-happy

- Hyphens make a two-word adjective before a noun, but not after it.

  Baxter Black, a former large-animal veterinarian, is a humorist and poet.
  Baxter Black, the humorist and poet, was formerly a veterinarian for large animals.

  Balloons as a means of flying were a late eighteenth-century invention.
  Balloons were a means of flying in the late eighteenth century.

- Hyphens have enjoyed a comeback with the vocabulary of the electronic world, for example, with *e-text* and *e-filing*. However, hyphens tend to disappear with frequent use. The hyphen is already optional in some cases, as long as you are consistent within your document.

  email or e-mail

Note that there is no space before or after a hyphen.

53 APOSTROPHES

Most of the time, when you add an *s* to a word, you don't need an apostrophe. Use apostrophes for contractions and possessives.

Do not add an apostrophe; just add *s* or *es*.

- To make a plural

two bosses	three CDs	500 free passes
mid 1980s	thirty families	

- To a present-tense verb

He sees.   She says.   It talks.   Carol sings.

Add an apostrophe.

- To a contraction (the apostrophe replaces the missing letter)

doesn't = does not	it's = it is	that's = that is
don't	I'm	weren't
didn't	you're	what's

- To a possessive

the company's policy	a director's style	a good night's sleep
Gus's hair	children's toys	a family's history
Ms. Jones's opinion	women's room	today's world

If the word is plural and already ends with *s*, add an apostrophe after the *s*.

my accounts' total value (several accounts)
grandparents' beliefs

Pronouns in possessive form have no apostrophe.

its   hers   his   ours   theirs   yours

- Use an apostrophe for the plural of letters used as letters.

In this typeface, *q*'s and *g*'s are too similar.

54 QUOTATION MARKS

Use quotation marks for someone else's exact words, or for words or phrases that you discuss out of context.

Quotations in this chapter come from the following selection of *Robert's Rules of Order* by Henry M. Robert (1915):

> The object of *Rules of Order* is to assist an assembly to accomplish in the best possible manner the work for which it was designed. To do this it is necessary to restrain the individual somewhat, as the right of an individual, in any community, to do what he pleases, is incompatible with the interests of the whole. Where there is no law, but every man does what is right in his own eyes, there is the least of real liberty.

▶ PUNCTUATION BEFORE A QUOTATION

Here are three ways to lead into a quotation:

- For short quotations (a word or a phrase), don't use *"Robert's Rules of Order* says," and don't put a comma before the quotation. Simply use the writer's phrase as it fits smoothly into your sentence:

  > Robert finds it essential to "restrain the individual somewhat" for the sake of orderly discussion.

- Put a comma before the quotation marks if you use "he says." Put no comma if you use "he says that."

  > Robert says, "Where there is no law, but every man does what is right in his own eyes, there is the least of real liberty."

  > Robert says that "it is necessary to restrain the individual somewhat."

- Use a colon (:) before a quotation of a sentence or more. Be sure you have a complete statement before the colon. Don't use "he says."

In one sentence, Robert pulls together the philosophy behind his book: "Where there is no law, but every man does what is right in his own eyes, there is the least of real liberty."

▶ Punctuation After a Quotation

At the end of a quotation, the period or comma goes inside the quotation marks. Do not close the quotation marks as you move from one sentence to the next until the person's words end. Use one mark of punctuation to end your sentence—never two periods or a comma and a period.

Semicolons go outside of closing quotation marks.

Robert says, "It is necessary to restrain the individual somewhat"; nevertheless, he does so in the interest of "real liberty."

Question marks and exclamation marks go inside if the person quoted is asking or exclaiming. (If you are asking or exclaiming, the mark goes outside.)

"Have you mastered the ins and outs of *Robert's Rules of Order?*" the delegate asked.

What does Robert mean by "real liberty"?

▶ Indenting Long Quotations

Long quotations (more than three lines) do not get quotation marks. Instead, start on a new line and indent the whole left margin of the quotation. After the quotation, return to the original margin and continue your paragraph.

Henry Robert had thoughtfully considered the implications of his work:

To do this [conduct an effective meeting] it is necessary to restrain the individual somewhat . . . . Where there is no law, but every man does what is right in his own eyes, there is the least of real liberty.

Use brackets ([ ]) around a changed word or added explanation.

Use an ellipsis (three periods, with a space before and after each) to indicate an omission. If necessary, use a fourth period to end the sentence.

Use *sic*—"as it stood"—in brackets to indicate an error in the original.

> Jamiesen writes: "The principle [sic] effect is chaos."

▶ DIALOGUE

In dialogue, start a new paragraph every time you switch from one speaker to the other.

> A lively exchange ended the meeting:
>
> "I totally reject your conclusions! I am not convinced that this research is without bias!" S.B. shouted.
>
> "Not without the bias of your assumptions, you mean!" growled P.H.
>
> "This meeting is adjourned!" ruled the chair.

▶ WRITING ABOUT A WORD OR PHRASE

When you discuss a word or phrase, surround it with quotation marks.

> Advertisers use "America," while news reporters refer to "the United States."

Do not use quotation marks around slang; either use the word without quotation marks or find a better word.

▶ QUOTATION WITHIN A QUOTATION

For quotations within a quotation, use single quotation marks:

> According to radio announcer Rhingo Lake, "The jockey clearly screamed 'Foul!' as the horse fell to the ground right before the finish line."

▶ QUOTING POETRY

For poetry, when quoting two or more lines, indent from the left margin and copy the lines of poetry exactly as the poet arranged them.

> We are such stuff
>
> As dreams are made on; and our little life
>
> Is rounded with a sleep.

When quoting a few words of poetry that include a line break, use a slash mark to show where the poet's line ends.

> In *The Tempest*, Shakespeare calls us "such stuff/As dreams are made on. . . ."

When a line of poetry is too long to fit on a line in your document, indent the turnover line an additional three spaces, as in the following line from Walt Whitman's *Leaves of Grass*.

> I believe that a leaf of grass is no less than the journeywork
>   of the stars.

55 ITALICIZING (UNDERLINING) OR QUOTING TITLES

Italicize or underline titles of longer works; use quotation marks for titles of shorter works that are published within the longer works.

Longer Works

Italicize or <u>underline</u> titles of longer works, such as books, magazines, plays, newspapers, movies, and television programs.

Saturday Night Live	*War and Peace*
The Wall Street Journal	*The Wizard of Oz*

Don't mix underlining and italics for titles in the same document. In email, use the underline before and after the title.

The Art of Kissing, Tickling, and Being Bored.

Shorter Works

Put "quotation marks" around titles of shorter works, such as articles, chapter titles, poems, songs, and short stories.

"U.S. on Track for Surplus"   "The Star-Spangled Banner"

Remember that a comma or period, if needed, goes inside the quotation marks.

In "Talk, Type, Read E-Mail," Amy Harmon discusses the intricacies of juggling several tasks on the computer.

Special Cases

- Journalists use quotation marks for all titles; use that format for press releases and articles you submit to nonscholarly publications.

- Do not italicize or place quotation marks around your title on a cover sheet—unless your title contains someone else's title:

  Analysis of Salamander Population in Oxbow Tributary
  1999–2004

> Proposed Modifications to *Murder in the Tanning Salon,*
> Scene 7

Capitalize only the first word and all major words in a title.

- Do not italicize or quote names of groups or organizations. It is, however, optional to boldface a featured name (for example, in a promotional piece).

> **Thinc Design**   **The Beatles**

APPENDIX

SAMPLE BUSINESS DOCUMENTS
Memo

Bad News Memo

Detailed Email

Email Templates

Letter of Recommendation

Meeting Agenda

Press Release

Cover Letter for Résumé

Résumé (Emphasis on Accomplishments)

Résumé (Emphasis on Skills)

Résumé (Limited Experience—Concealing Current Employer)

Résumé (Significant Experience)

GUIDELINES FOR PREPARING DOCUMENTS
Basic Formatting for Business Documents

Shortcuts for "Word"

Grammar Review: Common Sentence Patterns

Anatomy of a Sentence: How to Diagram

A LIST OF IMPORTANT REFERENCES

SAMPLE MEMO

Bromelain
Research
Group

One Highview Drive,
Indianapolis, IN 46222

Date: Jan. 10, 2005

To: All Employees

From: Deana Bartlett   dbartlett@Bromelain.com
Executive Vice President   Phone   317.636.1500
Fax   317.636.1560

Re: Employee Stock Option Purchase Plan

To encourage stock ownership by employees of the Bromelain Research Group and its subsidiaries, the board of directors has adopted a new **Employee Stock Option Purchase Plan** (ESOPP). We expect stockholder approval of this plan by February 1, 2005, and that the Plan will become active by March 1, 2005.

The principal provision of ESOPP will be to offer all employees who work at least twenty hours per week an opportunity to purchase company stock through payroll deductions. The price at which the employee may purchase the stock is 85 percent of the last reported sale price of the BRG common stock on the day the offering period ends.

An employee may elect to have up to 10 percent of his or her salary deducted for the purpose of purchasing stock. In no event may an employee's total deduction or payment during a calendar year exceed $5000.

No person will be eligible to participate in ESOPP if he or she would be treated for tax purposes as possessing 5 percent or more of the voting power or value of BRG's common stock. The BRG Board of Directors retains the right to determine ineligibility of any employee, particularly those employees who are considered "highly compensated" by the company.

As of December 31, 2004, approximately 1730 persons were eligible to participate in ESOPP.

ESOPP will be administered by the Management Development and Compensation Committee, which is authorized to make rules and regulations for the administration and interpretation of the plans.

SAMPLE BAD NEWS MEMO

> **DELLMORE CORPORATION**
> 45678 Peachtree Avenue
> Atlanta, GA 30318

Date: April 8, 2005

To: Pramila Varda
Director, Interface Dept.

From: Jason C. Whitmore *JCW*   jcwhitmore@Dellmore.com
Vice President for Human Resources   Phone   404-355-2496
Fax   404-355-2497

Subject: Confirmation of Future Staffing Revisions

This memorandum specifies your department's staff reductions resulting from our recent merger with ISF.

As described during the December 4 meeting, the DellMore Corporation Executive Committee hopes to ensure the least disruptive adjustment to our recent merger. We are counting on you and the other directors to ease any problems resulting from the reduction of existing staff.

The merger requires the integration of our two interface departments. This consolidation will reduce DellMore's interface staff from twelve to seven individuals:

—Transfer or termination of two supervisors
—Transfer or termination of three level 2 technicians

We are very well aware of the difficulty of a transition like this. Every effort will be made to accommodate individual needs and to relocate staff within the new ISF corporation. In the next few weeks, Paul Mooney will be meeting with you to help you evaluate Interface Department staff. Meanwhile, please feel free to call Paul if you have particular questions or concerns.

We very much regret the hardship this reduction will entail. However, a reinvigorated DellMore within ISF will ultimately bring the greatest benefit to the greatest number of our employees.

cc: Paul Mooney, Director of Human Resources

Sample Detailed Email

From: Diana Wienbroer [DianaWienbroer@yahoo.com]

Sent: Monday, October 25, 2004 10:34 AM

To: Kiera Cunningham (kiera_cunningham@mcgraw-hill.com)

Subject: Design for *Rules of Thumb*

Kiera:

As I said on the phone, this is the cleanest, most attractive set of page designs we've ever seen. Many thanks for your care and creativity.

You have responded to nearly all of our issues. We have just a couple of remaining requests.

White Space

We would like more vertical space above subheadings. For example, page 10 of the layout sheets shows identical space above heads and paragraphs.

Titles and Headings

We particularly like the typefaces for the section titles and for subheadings. However page 37 is actually a new chapter; please change the headings and subheadings accordingly.

Thanks for your attention to our requests. For our part, we promise speedy responses during production.

Please call me if you have any questions.

Diana

Diana Roberts Wienbroer—also for Jay Silverman
tel/fax212.555.7039

SAMPLE TEMPLATES FOR REPLIES TO EMAIL

You can save time replying to routine emails by using a few templates. Be sure that your message closes with your full name, as well as the exact contact information you want the recipient to have, and that a copy also goes to anyone referred to in your message.

> Thank you for your message, repeated below. I am forwarding it to my [partner, colleague, assistant, supervisor], who will get back to you soon.
>
> person to contact   email address   telephone number
> [name and title]   [with hours of availability]
>
> We appreciate your business and will do everything possible to resolve this situation to your satisfaction.
>
> Sincerely.
>
> _____

> Thank you for your comments on my work.
>
> The volume of email I receive prohibits personal replies. However, I am grateful for your thoughts.
>
> Very truly yours.

Many email programs allow you to set up automatic replies to your email messages while you are out of the office. Here is a suggested format:

> I will be away from the office from [day, time, date] until [day, time, date].
>
> I will respond to your message upon my return.
>
> If you need an immediate reply, please email or call my [partner, colleague, assistant, supervisor].
>
> person to contact   email address   telephone number
> [name and title]   [with hours of availability]
>
> Best wishes.

SAMPLE LETTER OF RECOMMENDATION

Holly Sherman Peña ■ **Charter Systems Inc.** ■ **Austin, TX 78766**

April 18, 2005

Mr. Anthony Varricchio
Lincoln County Office Systems
P O Box 339
Diamondville, WY 83116

Re: Amy Tarns, Applicant for Office Manager

Dear Mr. Varricchio:

I am writing to recommend an exceptional candidate for your consideration. Amy Tarns would make a substantial contribution to your organization should you select her to be your office manager.

I have supervised Amy in her position as office manager at Charter Systems for the last seven years. Ours is a small firm specializing in installation of office systems—three partners and twenty or more part-timers. Amy's job is to coordinate and provide transition as the various part-timers submit reports, claims, and referrals to our company. Over the years, we have all benefited from Amy's organizational strategies and attention to detail.

Amy is supremely qualified for the position of office manager at your company.

- The first thing that you will notice about Amy is her energy and enthusiasm. Amy pays attention to people, is genuinely interested in their problems, and remembers them.

- Amy is an organizer, with an intuitive understanding of the simplest solution. She'll have everything in efficient order in record time. She will take a task (the company picnic, for example) and make it happen in a truly professional, fun way.

- On a personal note, Amy has strong values. She respects those around her; she has high expectations of her own performance (and is unflinching when wrongs need to be addressed; and she practices the golden rule.

Please feel free to call or write if you wish further information from me. I write in support of what will surely be a loss to us, but Amy and her husband are determined to move to your area, so I hope that you will welcome them.

Very truly yours,

Holly Peña

Holly Sherman Peña
Vice President, Charter Systems

hspena@chartersys.com ■ **Phone 512.572.6676** ■ **Fax 512.555.6677**

SAMPLE MEETING AGENDA

JDE AND ASSOCIATES / 1739 Ambar Drive / Calabasas, CA 91360

Interdepartmental Memo

Date: July 12, 2004

To: Jack Adams, Amy Fong, Woody Rainey, Juanita Valdez, and Ben Zapolski

From: Sheila Thomes   818-340-6666
             Director, Studio B   SThomes@JDEassoc.com

Subject: Final Meeting on Proposal for Sheffield Gardens
             Thursday, July 15, 2004, 10:00 a.m. PDT Conference Room 4

AGENDA

1. Approval of Minutes July 8, 2004, attached
2. Report from Juanita on revised test results
3. Report from Jack on section 16: bar graphs
4. Report from Sheila on printing and packaging
5. Approval of press release, attached
6. Discussion of final issues
   - Delivery of documents
   - Follow-through with Mr. Dolan

Please be prompt. I've arranged for coffee/tea at 9:45.
Let's try to adjourn by 1 p.m.

SAMPLE PRESS RELEASE

S E L K I R K   L A B S

Selkirk Labs, Inc. • Six Research Blvd. • Boulder, CO. 88999

PRESS RELEASE for distribution 11 a.m. MST, November 2, 2004

DISTRIBUTION: Business Editors
LENGTH: 186 words
HEADLINE: SELKIRK LABS TO ACQUIRE ARGO TECHNOLOGY
DATELINE: Boulder, CO, November 6, 2004

Selkirk Labs, a leading manufacturer of computer parts, agreed today to buy Argo Technology for $9.5 million in cash, thus beginning an expansion into the software business.

Under this agreement, made through Selkirk's SLI investment unit, Selkirk is to pay 32 percent more than the Friday closing price of Argo.

Argo Technology, a small software company based in Palo Alto, California, scored its first major market hit last year with its best-selling *Aware!,* a program designed to gather news from a wide variety of sources using each client's interests and preferences.

Cara Copland, spokesperson for Selkirk Labs, says this purchase "provides a major channel for our new commitment to service." The purchase represents the first acquisition in a program of planned expansion undertaken by Selkirk last year.

Argo will continue to operate as a separate subsidiary of Selkirk Labs but will move its offices to Boulder where Selkirk is located.

Negotiations are already underway for purchase of suitable property for Argo's new facility, now in final designing stages. Copland says Selkirk anticipates that the acquisition should be completed during the first quarter of 2005.

SELKIRK CONTACT: Bess Lanier
303.777.9077
Fax 303.777.9088
b_lanier@selkirk.com

ARGO CONTACT: Fred Elsasser
916.362.7033
Fax 916.384.3084
Felsass@ARGO.com

SAMPLE COVER LETTER FOR RÉSUMÉ

Joylene A. Bigelow
1805 Eisenhower Drive
Clinton, MS 39056
601-924-2892

February 14, 2005

Ms. Betty Taylor
Vice President for Human Resources
Kirtley Pharmaceuticals
3905 Chickasaw Drive
Jackson, MS 39216

Dear Ms. Taylor:

Jay Berman told me that Kirtley Pharmaceuticals plans to reorganize its training and development department and that you will soon be advertising for the new position of director of training.

As my résumé demonstrates, I have had a wide range of experience with staff development in the health-care industry. In particular, my recent experience at Omni-Group Health Plans has fully prepared me for the position you are creating. You will also find that my knowledge of the nursing home and insurance businesses can be an asset to Kirtley's sales agents, as will my personal knowledge of potential clients.

I began my professional career as a nurse, but I have found true fulfillment as a teacher/coach. My approach emphasizes how employees promote the public image of the organization—through being better informed, more caring, and more thorough than the competition. I know that concern about Kirtley's image has prompted your decision to reorganize, and I would appreciate the chance to help.

Should you be interested in discussing my ideas, I would be happy to meet with you at your earliest convenience.

Yours truly,

Joylene A. Bigelow

SAMPLE RÉSUMÉ (EMPHASIS ON ACCOMPLISHMENTS)

Joylene A. Bigelow
1805 Eisenhower Drive
Clinton, MS 39056
601-924-2892

Objective: A management position in the health-care industry

Experience

Dec. 1997–   Omni-Group Health Plans, Inc.
Jan. 2005   Director, Human Resources, Southern District Office

Hired, supervised, evaluated, scheduled, and managed a staff of 175–200 claims adjustors, accountants, and review panelists for the Claims Division of this regional office of a national comprehensive health insurance company. I also provided initial and ongoing training/education for the staff. In 1995, I developed policies and procedures for streamlining our response to clients' contested claims.

June 1992–   Director of Nursing
Nov. 1997   Vicksburg Trace Haven

Trace Haven is a 120-bed nursing facility with a 22-bed SNF. I was responsible for interviewing, hiring, firing, supervising, and scheduling a staff of over seventy employees. I attended therapy meetings, developed forms and protocols, provided training, reviewed potential residents, and oversaw implementation of state regulations governing nursing facilities.

April 1991– Staff Nurse
May 1992   ParkView Home Health

Conducted skilled nursing visits and completed required documentation of care. Successfully introduced a system whereby each nurse's assignment was made according to his or her caseload—not randomly as it had been in the past.

SAMPLE RÉSUMÉ (CONTINUED)

Joylene A. Bigelow, page 2

Education

Bilingual (English-Spanish)

1977   Diploma in Nursing

Graduated with honors from a three-year diploma program at Mercy Hospital–Street Memorial School of Nursing, Vicksburg, and passed the State Board for Examination of Nurses with commendation.

1977–1982   In-Service Training

During these years, I worked in a variety of jobs in hospitals, research, a comprehensive health center, and the Mississippi State Hospital at Whitfield. I participated in numerous job-specific classes covering such topics as wound care, hypertension, diabetes, management of people, interpersonal skills, nursing documentation, supervising difficult employees, time management, and so on.

Note: From 1982–1991, I took time out from my profession to marry and raise two children. However, during those years I continued to develop skills relevant to my professional responsibilities.

Additional Accomplishments

1990–1997   Chair of the Visitation Committee, All Angels Church

Responsible for coordinating parishioners' visits to the ill, infirm, and bereaved. I developed a network of volunteers who communicate via a simple phone chain to supplement the visits by the clergy.

1988–1992   Coordinator for Welcome Wagon Services for the
                    Vicksburg area

Duties included training volunteer greeters, soliciting donations from area merchants, and computerizing the system for registry of new area residents.

1983–1989   Volunteer Fundraiser, Annual Red Cross Fund Drive

Each year, for approximately six weeks, I recruited and trained volunteers to solicit donations. My team surpassed its funding goal each time.

SAMPLE RÉSUMÉ (EMPHASIS ON SKILLS)

Joylene A. Bigelow
1805 Eisenhower Drive
Clinton, MS 39056
601-924-2892

Objective: A management position in human resources

Qualifications

Management Skills

- Interviewed, hired, supervised, scheduled, and terminated staff in health-care organizations with up to 200 employees
- Developed policies and procedures, forms, and protocols
- Oversaw implementation of state regulations governing nursing facilities

Training Skills

- Provided initial and ongoing training/education for staff at insurance company and nursing home
- Recruited and trained volunteers for Welcome Wagon and Red Cross

Organizational Skills

- Developed a system for equalizing nursing assignments in a high-quality home nursing organization
- Coordinated and developed a system to enable volunteers to visit church members in need

Education

1977   Honors Diploma in Nursing
              Mercy Hospital–Street
              Memorial School of Nursing,
              Vicksburg, MS

Certification, State Board for Examination of Nurses with commendation,

Bilingual (English-Spanish)

Sample Résumé (Continued)

Work History

Dec. 1997– **Jan. 2005–**	Omni-Group Health Plans, Inc. Director, Human Resources, Southern District
June 1992– **Nov. 1997**	Director of Nursing Vicksburg Trace Haven Nursing Home
1990–1997	Chair of the Visitation Committee All Angels Church, Vicksburg
April 1991– **May 1992**	Staff Nurse ParkView Home Health
1988–1992	Coordinator, Welcome Wagon Services Vicksburg and environs
1983–1989	Volunteer Fundraiser Annual Red Cross Fund Drive
1977–1983	A variety of jobs in hospitals, research, a comprehensive health center, and the Mississippi State Hospital at Whitfield

SAMPLE RÉSUMÉ (LIMITED EXPERIENCE— CONCEALING CURRENT EMPLOYER)

Michael J. Waite   •

589 Brookview Road

St. Louis, MO 65790

voice mail 408.999.3453   email waitemj@yahoo.com

Objective: To design information technology that really works in the workplace

Employment

June 2003–present
(firm supplying the St. Louis area with personalized installation and service for intranets)

On-site programmer and trouble-shooter. Modified, installed, and maintained personalized software for clients—many in high-data industries with systems of over 100 workstations. Acquired skills in solving problems quickly as well as meeting a variety of business client needs.

1997–2003 (summers only)
Radio Shack, St. Louis, MO

Sales associate. Also assisted in electronic repairs. Acquired skills in dealing with customers and in solving simple mechanical problems.

Education

1997–2003 University of Vermont B.S. in Computer Technology

Dean's list. Volunteer 1999–2002 (three hours weekly, twelve weeks per semester, seven semesters) training senior citizens in computer use.

Also provided maintenance to computer systems in local public schools.

1993–1997 Washington High School, St. Louis, MO

Academic diploma. Odyssey of the Mind [intellectual teamwork competitions], three years; state finalist 1994. Senior Master Project: created an interactive computer game, "MouseHole." Baseball Varsity, three years.

References and program samples available upon request.

SAMPLE RÉSUMÉ (SIGNIFICANT EXPERIENCE)

Carolyn Dunn
80 Crozier Road
Kent, CT 06934
860-378-3242   c3866@aol.com

1999–present	Freelance Television Producer
1991–1999	Bozell Advertising Worldwide, Inc. New York, NY Vice President Executive Producer
1986–1991	Saatchi & Saatchi Worldwide, Inc. New York, NY Executive Vice President Director, Broadcast Operations
1982–1986	DDB Needham Worldwide, Inc. New York, NY Senior Vice President Director, Broadcast Production
1978–1982	Needham Worldwide, Inc. Los Angeles, CA Senior Vice President Director, Broadcast Production
1974–1978	Steppingstone Productions, Inc. New York, NY Executive Producer President and Owner

Manhattanville College
Purchase, NY
B.A. Degree

Basic Formatting for Business Documents

The visual presentation of your documents communicates your sense of professionalism. Check other sections of this appendix for models of the traditional formats for letters, memos, agendas, and résumés.

PAPER

- Standard 8.5 × 11-inch white paper is always correct. If using tinted stationery, make sure that it allows for easy reading of standard typefaces.

- For multiple pages, staple once or clip in the upper left-hand corner. When binding is necessary, make sure that the finished document is easy to handle and that the margins have been adjusted to accommodate the binding.

TYPEFACE

- Use a No. 12 typeface in an easy-to-read font such as Arial or Times New Roman.

- Do not use all capital letters, all boldface, or all italics.

MARGINS

- Use an inch to an inch-and-a-half margin on all four sides. If the document will be bound, adjust the top or left margin accordingly.

- Begin each paragraph at the left margin.

- For most documents, do not justify (line up the margin) on the right, which distorts the spacing between letters and words, making the document harder to read.

SPACING

- Single-space throughout and double-space between paragraphs.
- Use the print preview function to check vertical spacing. With letters and memos, you can add space between elements for better vertical centering.

PUNCTUATION

- Leave two spaces after
  periods   exclamation marks   question marks
- Leave one space after
  commas   semicolons   colons
- Use the one-em dash—or two hyphens—with no space before or after.
- Make an ellipsis (. . .) by using three periods with a space before and after each period.
- Never begin a line with a period or a comma.
- Never put a space before a punctuation mark (except for an ellipsis or an opening parenthesis).

DIVIDING WORDS

Avoid, as much as possible, dividing a word from one line to the next. If you must divide a very long word, divide only between syllables. To find the syllables, look up the word in a dictionary. It will be printed with dots between the syllables: ex · per · i · men · ta · tion. Never divide a one-syllable word, like *brought*. Never divide a word after only one letter.

PAGE NUMBERS

Number each page after the first. To avoid inserting the page number on the first page, specify "different header for first page" in the page setup>layout in "Word."

COVER SHEET OR TITLE PAGE

You may decide to develop a recognizable design for your covers, using heavier paper with your company logo and appropriate graphics. However, the format for a title page can also be used for a cover sheet.

- Center the title, without quotation marks or underlining, in the middle of the page.

- Place your contact information in the lower right-hand corner.

SHORTCUTS FOR "WORD"

Here are some tips to save time when you are using *Microsoft Word*, the most commonly used word-processing program. Some of these tips also work in other programs.

▶ SETTING UP THE DOCUMENT

To insert the current date	Insert Menu > Date and Time
To add page numbers	Insert Menu > Page Numbers
To add a header to each page	View Menu > Header and Footer; type your header into the box
To align your header on the right	Ctrl + R
To avoid numbering your first page	File Menu > Page Setup > Layout; click "different header for first page"
To center your title	Ctrl + E
To set the margins for the whole document or for just a selection	File Menu > Page Setup > Margins
To single space	Ctrl + 1
To double space	Ctrl + 2
To customize your toolbar	Right-click on a blank section of the toolbar; click "customize"
To set paragraph indentations	Format Menu>Paragraph> Indents and Spacing > Indentations > Left > 0.5" Special > first line

To set a hanging indent for a bibliography or reference page	Format Menu > Paragraph > Indents and Spacing > Special Hanging By > 0.5"

USING THE RULER (AT THE TOP OF THE PAGE)

The upper marker on the left of the ruler sets the left margin for the first line of each paragraph; the lower marker sets the left margin for the second and any following lines.

▼ · · · | · · · 1
▲
■

To set paragraph indentations	Click and slide the upper marker to the half-inch point, leaving the lower marker at the left margin
To form a hanging indent for a bibliography or reference page ▼ · · ·	· · · 1 ▲ ■	Click and slide the lower marker to the half-inch point, leaving the upper marker at the left margin

A mouseclick at any point on the ruler can set a tab (marked with a little *L*).

USING AUTOCORRECT (SET THIS UP BEFORE YOU TYPE)

To automatically correct errors	Tools Menu > AutoCorrect; you usually make check "Replace text as you type"; then modify the list that follows
To insert a specific word or phrase whenever you type its abbreviation	Tools Menu > AutoCorrect; check "Replace text as you type"; then type in the abbreviation and the word to replace it—for example, "Replace *enx* with *environmentally friendly*"

Warning: Be careful to use a unique abbreviation (such as one with an x); asking AutoCorrect to replace *env* with *environmentally friendly* throughout your document would create a disaster. You may also find it helpful to keep a list of your abbreviations.

▶ TYPING AND EDITING

To hide the red wavy lines (Spelling) or the green wavy lines (Grammar)	Tools Menu > Options > Spelling and Grammar > Hide . . . errors
To add to your custom dictionary	Tools Menu > AutoCorrect > Exceptions
To locate all instances of an error and replace it with the word or words you specify	Edit Menu > Find (**or** Ctrl + F); type the word or phrase you want to change; then click on *Replace* and type the word or phrase you prefer
To check for repetition of points or overuse of certain words	Edit Menu > Find (**or** Ctrl + F); type the word or phrase you want to see
To prevent unwanted text color (for example, with downloaded material)	Format Menu > Font > Font color; select black instead of automatic color
To edit hyperlinks	Right-click and select the option—such as "Remove Hyperlink" (to return a web address to a regular font)
To mark changes as you revise	Tools > track changes (**or** Ctrl + Shift + E)
To insert a comment	Insert > comment (**or** Alt + Ctrl +M)

WORKING WITH GRAPHICS

To wrap text around inserted graphics	Right-click on the graphic; Format picture > Layout
To adjust the size of the text box	Click on the borderlines and drag
To adjust the position of the highlighted image	Drag it, or press Ctrl + one of the arrow keys

▶ USING KEYBOARD SHORTCUTS

You probably already use a few keyboard shortcuts—such as Ctrl + S to save or Ctrl + P to print. Check "keys" under the Help menu to find other two- or three-key combinations to perform the functions you do frequently.

MANEUVERS FOR THE ENTIRE DOCUMENT

To undo a change	Ctrl + Z
To redo after undoing	Ctrl + Y
To go to the last change	Shift + F5
To turn on /turn off tracking function (for showing editing changes)	Ctrl + Shift + E
To get out of a frozen program	Ctrl + Alt + Delete
To close a program	Alt + F4
To use the spellchecker	F7
To delete one word to the left	Ctrl + Backspace
To delete one word to the right	Ctrl + Delete
To search for text or formatting	Ctrl + F

To insert a comment	Alt + Ctrl+ M
To move within preview page while zoomed in	arrow keys
To toggle between programs	Alt + Tab

HIGHLIGHT THE SELECTION BEFORE USING THESE SHORTCUTS

(Double-click on the mouse to highlight a word; triple-click to highlight a paragraph.)

To change capitalization	Shift + F3
To increase font size	Ctrl +]
To decrease font size	Ctrl + [
To open Font menu (to change format)	Ctrl + D
To add/remove underline	Ctrl + U
To add/remove bold	Ctrl + B
To add/remove italics	Ctrl + I

USE THESE SHORTCUTS ON THE WEB

Some of the shortcuts above will also work while you're surfing with your browser. Here are some more:

To refresh the screen	F5
To review the the sites you have visited (history)	Ctrl + H
To add the current website to your favorites	Ctrl + D
To keep the original website window open when you click on a link	hold down shift key as you click

► SWITCHING BETWEEN MAC AND WINDOWS

Mac		*Windows*
The Command key ⌘	=	Windows Ctrl key
The Option key	=	Windows Alt key
Mac mouse button	=	left button on Windows mouse
Mac mouse button + Command key	=	right button on Windows mouse (for information on the selection or to give other options)
To close the window: see upper left of screen		see upper right of the screen

FILE SHARING

Macs can read most Windows files. However, when receiving an email attachment that has been created by a Mac, Windows users will need to add a three-letter extension (such as .doc or .jpg) to the file name before saving the download.

GRAMMAR REVIEW: COMMON SENTENCE PATTERNS

Although simple sentences are often the most effective, good writing uses a variety of sentence patterns. Combine sentences to vary the rhythm or to show the interrelationship of several ideas.

▶ SIMPLE SENTENCES

Each simple sentence contains a subject and a verb, which form the kernel of the sentence. Usually, a completer (a complement, direct object, or modifier) is added.

To control grammar, punctuation, and style, first identify the verb and then its subject. At the heart of every sentence—no matter how complicated—is a subject and a verb.

> We will move.
>
> Money talks.
>
> The delivery is late.

We, money, and *delivery* are the subjects; *will move, talks,* and *is* are the verbs. Notice that the verb enables the subject to do or be something. Strong writing features the verb—usually early in the sentence.

- In a command or a direction, the subject is understood to be "you"—the reader.

  > Avoid submerging this product in water.
  >
  > Walk two blocks past the traffic light.

- Sentences can have more than one subject and more than one verb:

  > Both our accountant and our marketing manager will attend the conference.
  > (two subjects—*accountant* and *manager*)

The designers will analyze your reception area and offer three new options.
(two verbs—*analyze* and *offer*)

- Usually a word or phrase completes the subject and verb:

    Taneeka Moore supervises fifty-three auditors.

    It's not very difficult.

    This report says absolutely nothing.

    Regina swims every morning.

- Sometimes a word or group of words introduces the main part of a sentence:

    However, the entertainment expenses have been disallowed.

    For example, we use only organic produce.

    In the packet labeled "Open First," you'll find the necessary tools.

▶ COMPOUND SENTENCES

You can join two related sentences with a comma plus a coordinating conjunction, or with a semicolon. The result gives equal weight to the point each sentence makes.

COMMA PLUS COORDINATING CONJUNCTION

A coordinating conjunction establishes a specific relationship between two sentences.

Sentence, [coordinating conjunction] sentence.

Coordinating Conjunctions

and   but   or   nor   for   so   yet

I prefer the French wallpaper, but Margaret doesn't care for it.

I prefer the French wallpaper, so that's what I'm ordering.

I prefer the French wallpaper, yet I'm open to other patterns.

Note that without the coordinating conjunction, the comma is inadequate; a semicolon is then required.

SEMICOLON

A semicolon can be used instead of a period between two closely related sentences.

Sentence; *sentence.*

I prefer the French wallpaper; it is within our budget.

The committee recommends Bruce Urquhart; our explanation is attached.

CONJUNCTIVE ADVERBS

Often, a transition word—a conjunctive adverb—is used to provide smoothness following a semicolon. A comma before these words is not sufficient to join two sentences.

however   therefore   thus   nevertheless   indeed   then   besides

I prefer the French wallpaper; besides, it is within our budget.

I prefer the French wallpaper; however, Margaret doesn't care for it.

Sometimes, instead of joining two sentences, a conjunctive adverb is tucked within a sentence.

Margaret, however, doesn't care for the French wallpaper.

The decision, therefore, is irrevocable.

The Internet, nevertheless, is the primary vending market for this product.

Here, the conjunctive adverbs are surrounded by commas.

▶ COMPLEX OR SUBORDINATE SENTENCES

Two sentences can be joined if one is preceded by a subordinating word.

[*Subordinating Word*] *sentence, sentence.*

Sentence [*subordinating word*] *sentence.*

Subordinating Words

because   although   if   whereas   when   before   after   while

A complex sentence has two parts:

* A main sentence—a complete sentence that can stand alone

* A subordinated sentence—a sentence introduced by a subordinating word and which, therefore, cannot stand alone

> The primary market for sea urchins is Japan although they are harvested in Maine.

Notice that the parts are reversible.

> Although they are harvested in Maine, the primary market for sea urchins is Japan.

Note that when the subordinating word is in the middle, no comma is necessary.

> When the annual reports arrive from the printer, they must be stored temporarily in the conference room.

> The annual reports must be stored temporarily in the conference room when they arrive from the printer.

> After the morning conference ends, we'd be pleased to have you as guests for lunch.

> We'd be pleased to have you as guests for lunch after the morning conference ends.

▶ COMPOUND-COMPLEX SENTENCES

A compound-complex sentence occurs when one or both halves of a compound sentence have subordinated parts.

> Although we had heard some unpleasant rumors, we planned to sign the contract; but we canceled when the truth came out.

> The piano has to be moved onto the stage a day ahead of time so it can be tuned twenty-four hours before the concert begins.

ANATOMY OF A SENTENCE: HOW TO DIAGRAM

Try diagramming a troublesome sentence to figure out what modifies what.

When you can't fix a problem sentence, analyzing how the parts connect can help you see where the trouble is. You can map out (diagram) the structure of your sentence. When you find a place for all the parts as you have written them, you can discover

- the parts that need to be rearranged

- the parts that need to be rephrased

- the parts (perhaps even whole sentences) that should be separated or dropped

Here are the basic techniques for diagramming, followed by several diagrammed sentences.

HOW TO DIAGRAM

- Write the subject, verb, and object (or complement) on a horizontal line.

- Draw a vertical line (through the horizontal line) to divide the subject and verb.

- Draw a short vertical line (which stops at the horizontal line) before the direct object.

- Draw a line leaning back to the subject before the complement.

- Write modifiers on horizontal lines under the word they modify.

- Separate the preposition from its object with a short vertical line.

- Use horizontal parallel lines for parallel parts—plural subjects, verbs, clauses, and so on.

- Use a horizontal line raised on a carat (^) for phrases or clauses that *as a unit* serve as subject or object.

Samples of Diagramming

Marlon deserves a promotion.

Marlon | deserves | promotion
                        a

Marlon is the subject; *deserves* is the verb; *promotion* is the direct object; *a* modifies *promotion*.

This disk is full.

disk | is \ full
This

Disk is the subject; *is* is the verb; *full* is the complement; *this* modifies *disk*.

We will close early on Tuesday.

We is the subject; *will close* is the verb; *early* and the prepositional phrase *on Tuesday* modify *will close*.

Turkeys and white-tailed deer roam freely in Lebanon Township.

Turkeys and *deer* are the subjects; *and* is the conjunction that joins them; *white-tailed* modifies *deer*; *roam* is the verb; *freely* modifies *roam*; the prepositional phrase *in Lebanon Township* also modifies *roam*.

Samples of Diagramming (Continued)

Our goal is to serve the tastiest salads in the city.

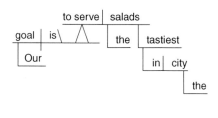

Goal is the subject; *is* is the verb; the complement that modifies the subject *goal* is an infinitive phrase—*to serve the tastiest salads in the city.* *To serve* is the infinitive; *salads* is its object; *the* and *tastiest* modify *salads*.

If you accept the new rental space, we will pay for all moving expenses.

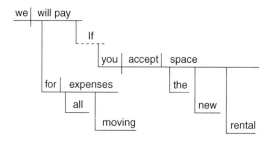

In the main sentence, *we* is the subject; *will pay* is the verb; *for expenses* modifies the verb, and *all* and *moving* modify *expenses*. Subordinated to the main sentence is the first sentence, connected by *if*. In the subordinated sentence, *you* is the subject; *accept* is the verb, and *the*, *new*, and *rental* modify *space*.

A LIST OF IMPORTANT REFERENCES

Internet addresses listed here are regularly updated on our website:

> http://www.writingshortcuts.com/

Every day, more resources are available online. Your local library may offer software and passwords so you can access major databases free from your home or office; your business organization may provide additional access. However, even when a fee is required at a particular site, often it applies only to the ordering of a specific document. You may be able to get what you need by logging on and checking the free pages.

Your writing needs may require you to visit a library, subscribe regularly to professional journals, and/or buy key reference books, CDs, and DVDs. Check this list for some suggestions.

The following list does not separate resources according to format because the publication of material is gradually changing from print to digital. There is an advantage to each version; you may prefer to download and print information, work with it, and then return to the computer.

HELP WITH CREATIVITY AND WRITER'S BLOCK

Hughes, Elaine Farris. *Writing from the Inner Self.* New York: HarperCollins, 1991. Offers techniques and advice to free your creative, real self. This book is particularly helpful if you have to produce fresh, innovative material regularly.

Schneider, Pat. *Writing Alone and with Others.* New York: Oxford Univ. Press, 2003. Excellent advice for journal-keeping and for gaining confidence as a writer. Schneider also offers guidance for writing groups.

Ueland, Brenda. *If You Want to Write: A Book about Art, Independence and Spirit.* 2nd ed. Saint Paul, MN: Graywolf, 1987. Shows how to come up with ideas, find your unique voice, and write honestly.

A classic since the first edition (1938), this book encourages writing for its value to the writer—not merely as a job.

HELP WITH STYLE, GRAMMAR, AND USAGE

Booher, Dianna. *Good Grief, Good Grammar: A Business Person's Guide to Grammar and Usage.* New York: Fawcett, 1990. An easy-to-use, detailed guide to grammatical terms and their applications—for example, when to use *since* rather than *because.*

Burchfield, R. W., ed. *The New Fowler's English Usage.* 3rd ed. New York: Oxford, 2000. A thorough coverage of word usage.

Punctuation Made Simple
http://www.stpt.usf.edu/pms/

Strunk, William, Jr., and E. B. White. *The Elements of Style.* 3rd ed. New York: Macmillan, 1979. The classic—designed to help you write more elegantly. However, it assumes that you understand grammatical terms. The e-text is available at http://www.bartleby.com/141/

The Word Monger. Online newsletter addressing issues of writing professionally.
http://www.alexcommunications.com/newsletter.htm#top

HELP WITH DESIGNING ELECTRONIC DOCUMENTS

Lynch, Patrick J., and Sarah Horton. *Basic Design Principles for Creating Web Sites.* New Haven, CT: Yale University Press, 2001.

_____. *Web Style Guide,* 2nd ed. http://www.webstyleguide.com/

Norman, Donald A. *The Design of Everyday Things.* New York: Basic Books, 2002.

Tufte, Edward. *The Cognitive Style of PowerPoint.* Cheshire, CT: Graphics, 2003.

_____. *Envisioning Information.* Cheshire, CT: Graphics, 1990. http://www.edwardtufte.com/

Usability. U.S. Dept. of Health and Human Services Resource Page with guidelines and links to books and articles on design. http://usability.gov/

Virtual Library's Information Quality Page
http://www.ciolek.com/WWWVL-InfoQuality.html

Web Developer's Virtual Library
http://www.wdvl.com/

Williams, Robin, and John Tollett. *The Non-Designer's Web Book.* Berkeley, CA: Peachpit, 2004.

WWWConsortium(W3c). http://www.w3.org/

HELP WITH DETAILS FOR PUBLISHING AND DOCUMENTING RESEARCH

American Psychological Association. *Publication Manual of the American Psychological Association,* 5th ed. Washington, DC: APA, 2001. This manual describes the format used by publications in the natural and social sciences. http://www.apastyle.org/fifthchanges.html

Chicago Manual of Style. 15th ed. Chicago: University of Chicago Press, 2003. The most comprehensive and definitive of the style books for publishing. Use these guidelines if you are not committed to the requirements of a particular discipline. http://www.chicagomanualofstyle.org/tools.html

Council of Biology Editors. *Scientific Style and Format: The CBE Manual for Authors, Editors, and Publishers.* 6th ed. Washington, DC: American Institute of Biological Sciences, 1994. The 7th edition is in preparation. Meanwhile, updates can be found at http://www.councilscienceeditors.org/publications/ssf_7th.cfm/. Also see the Council of Biology Editors' website at http://www.cbe.org.cbe/

Dodd, Janet S. *The ACS Style Guide: A Manual for Authors and Editors.* 2nd ed. New York: Oxford Univ. P, 1997. Also see the American Chemical Society's website at http://www.acs.org/

Gibaldi, Joseph. *MLA Style Manual and Guide to Scholarly Publishing.* 2nd ed. New York: Modern Language Association, 1998. A guide for all the fine points for publications in foreign languages and in English literature.
http://www.mla.org/style_faq/

HELP WITH ENGLISH AS A SECOND LANGUAGE

Allen, Edward Jay. *Advanced American Idioms.* Language Development Series, 1982.

Ammer, Christine. *American Heritage Dictionary of Idioms.* Boston: Houghton, 2003. A good and full explanation of the meaning of phrases and when to use which preposition in a phrase.

Education Resources on the Internet
http://www.edufind.com/english/grammar/toc.cfm/

Spears, Richard A., ed. *NTC's American Idiom Dictionary.* New York: McGraw-Hill, 2000.

DICTIONARIES

American Heritage Dictionary. Contains excellent photographs and illustrations.

Foreign Word: Online Dictionaries and Free Translation Tools
http://www.foreignword.com/

Free Translation
http://www.freetranslation.com/

Google Translations
http://www.google.com/language_tools/

Merriam Webster Collegiate Dictionary. 11th ed. Springfield, MA: Merriam-Webster, 2003.

Merriam-Webster Dictionary
http://www.m-w.com/

Oxford English Dictionary (OED). 13 vols. Gives the full historical development of English words. See also *Concise Oxford English Dictionary,* 10th ed. New York: Oxford, 2002.

Roget's International Thesaurus of English Words and Phrases. 5th ed. New York: Addison Wesley, 1994. Also at http://humanities.uchicago.edu/orgs/ARTFL/forms_unrest/ROGET.html

Thesaurus from Reference.com http://thesaurus.reference.com/

Webster's New Universal Unabridged Dictionary of the English Language. 3rd ed. New York: Barnes & Noble, 2003. The dictionary most often cited.

To access the dictionary or thesaurus in your word-processing program, first highlight the word and then click your right mouse button.

ENCYCLOPEDIAS

In addition to the sources listed here, look for encyclopedias devoted to a particular subject—for example, there is a *Baseball Encyclopedia.* (Palmer & Gillette, eds. New York: Barnes & Noble, 2004).

Collier's Encyclopedia. Good general information source for contemporary subjects.

Encyclopedia Americana. Good for scientific and technical topics.

Encyclopedia Britannica (in print, on CD, or online for a fee). The most definitive, comprehensive encyclopedia. Annual supplement, *Britannica Book of the Year.* Also at http://www.britannica.com/

Free Internet Encyclopedia. http://www.cam-info.net/enc.html

STATISTICAL SOURCES

Most of the statistical sources listed here are also available in print under the same titles, in the reference sections of libraries.

American Statistical Index	http://www.fedstats.gov/
Bureau of Census Reports	http://www.census.gov/
Bureau of Labor Statistics	http://stats.bls.gov/
National Center for Health Statistics	http://www.cdc.gov/nchs/
Statistical Resources on the Web	http://www.lib.umich.edu/ govdocs/statsnew/
World Fact Book	http://www.bartleby.com/151/ http://www.odci.gov/cia/ publications/factbook/ index.html

See also the websites of individual federal agencies.

QUOTATIONS ORGANIZED BY SUBJECT

Bartlett's Familiar Quotations. 17th ed. Boston: Little, Brown, 2003. Also available on software or at http://www.columbia.edu/acis/bartleby/bartlett/

Metcalf, Fred. *The Penguin Dictionary of Modern Humorous Quotations.* New York: Penguin, 2002.

Oxford Dictionary of Quotations. New York: Oxford, 1999. See various editions on humorous quotations, modern quotations, and so forth.

The Quotations Page http://www.quotationspage.com/

Quote World http://www.quoteworld.org/

REFERENCE PAGES

Most library home pages offer access to a choice of databases. Subscribers often can access these from home as well, although some databases may be available only at designated terminals in the library. Librarians can advise you about reference guides and specialized databases for your particular subject.

The reference pages here list resources available on the web, and many also give research tips.

Business Connections from the New York Times	http://www.nytimes.com/library/cyber/reference/busconn.html
Business Reference Services, Library of Congress	http://www.loc.gov/rr/business/
Environment	http://www.envirolink.org/ http://www.earthwatch.org/
Federal Information Network	http://www.fedworld.gov/
Government Science Portal (links to government-sponsored sites)	http://www.science.gov/
Internet Public Library	http://www.ipl.org/
Itools	http://www.itools.com/
Librarians' Index to the Internet	http://lii.org/
Library of Congress Research Tools	http://lcweb.loc.gov/rr/tools.html
RefDesk (Virtual ReferenceDesk)	http://www.refdesk.com/
Resource Shelf for News Information Professionals	http://resourceshelf.freepint.com/
Scicentral Links to Worldwide Sources for Science News	http://www.scicentral.com/
U.S. Congress on the Internet (Congressional decisions)	http://thomas.loc.gov/
Writers' Free Reference Page	http://www.writers-free-reference.com/

SEARCH TOOLS FOR THE INTERNET

Be sure to use several different search engines—or use a metasearcher, which connects to a number of search engines simultaneously. However, the most efficient searches on the web rarely find chapters in books or articles in journals. For those, you will need the databases your library provides.

About.com
(each area is maintained by an expert whom you can email)

http://www.about.com/

AltaVista
(one of the most comprehensive, allows for sophisticated advanced searches)

http://altavista.com/

Dogpile
(fun to use, simultaneously searches several search engines, including Google)

http://www.dogpile.com/

Google
(huge database, retrieves at a high level of relevance)

http://www.google.com/

Highway 61
(simultaneously searches the twelve most popular search engines, arranging results by relevance)

http://www.highway61.com/

Hotbot
(allows for specifying words that appear only in the title, body, or links; can search in thirty-five languages)

http://www.hotbot.com/

Isleuth Web Directory and Search Engine
(includes phone directories)

http://www.isleuth.com/

List of additional metasearchers and their descriptions

http://www.wrx.zen.co.uk/meta2.htm

Search.com (fast and thorough metasearcher)	http://www.search.com/ search.html
Webcrawler (one of the fastest metasearchers)	http://webcrawler.com/
Yahoo (very fast search of a huge database)	http://www.yahoo.com/

BOOKS ONLINE

The following services provide free access to entire books originally in print. You can use a search engine to find other sites that offer more recent books online—for a fee.

Bartleby: Great Books Online	http://www.bartleby.com/
Bible on Line	http://www.biblegateway.com/
The Complete Works of William Shakespeare	http://the-tech.mit.edu/ Shakespeare/works.html
EServer	http://eserver.org/books/
Gutenberg	http://www.gutenberg.net/
Online Books Page at the University of Pennsylvania	http://onlinebooks.library. upenn.edu/

NEWS SOURCES ONLINE

Most news organizations and publications maintain a website with at least some material from their current issues or programs. Sources listed here allow free searches through their archives, although there may be a fee for the article itself.

BBC	http://www.bbc.co.uk/
Christian Science Monitor (complete issues since 1980)	http://www.csmonitor.com/

CNN	http://www.cnn.com/
National Public Radio	http://www.npr.org/
Newslink (links to magazines and newspapers)	http://newslink.org/
Newspapers.com	http://www.newspapers.com/
Los Angeles Times	http://www.latimes.com/
New York Times	http://www.nytimes.com/
Public Broadcasting System	http://www.pbs.org/
Salon (e-magazine)	http://www.salon.com/
Slate (e-magazine)	http://www.slate.com/
Total News (search engine for news posted on the web)	http://www.totalnews.com/
Washington Post	http://www.washingtonpost. com/
Wired	http://www.wired.com/

GENERAL REFERENCE BOOKS

This list includes a number of sources for off-beat information—to help you to think about problems in different ways, or to spark up a talk, or to add interesting filler to a newsletter.

Adams, Cecil. *Triumph of the Straight Dope.* New York: Random House, 1999. The latest book in a series from Adams's newspaper column "The Straight Dope," answering odd questions, such as "How many square inches of skin are on the average human body?" Searchable database at http://www.straightdope.com/

Ash, Russell. *The Book of 1001 Lists*. New York: Barnes & Noble, 2003.

Bragonia, Reginald, Jr., and David Fisher. *What's What: A Visual Glossary*. New York: Smithmark, 1994. Illustrates and names the parts of common objects.

Brewer's Dictionary of Phrase and Fable. 15th ed. New York: HarperCollins, 1995.

Burnam, Tom. *The Dictionary of Misinformation: The Book to Set the Record Straight*. New York: HarperCollins, 1986.

Ciardi, John. *A Browser's Dictionary: A Compendium of Curious Expressions and Intriguing Facts*. 2nd ed. New York: Harper & Row, 1983.

DeGregorio, William H., and Connie Jo Dickerson. *The Complete Book of U.S. Presidents*. New York: Random House, 1997.

Fadiman, Clifton, ed. *Bartlett's Book of Anecdotes*. New York: Little, Brown, 2000.

Feldman, David. *Life's Imponderables: The Solution to the Mysteries of Everyday Life*. New York: Barnes & Noble, 2003. Latest in a series, organized by questions and answers, but with indexes. See also *Do Penguins Have Knees? How Does Aspirin Find a Headache? How Do Astronauts Scratch an Itch?* and so forth.

Folkard, Claire, ed. *The Guinness Book of World Records*. New York: Bantam, 2004 (updated each year). Also look for Guinness books on records in aircraft, the Olympics, and sports.

Grun Bernard. *Timetables of History*. 3rd ed. New York: Simon & Schuster, 1991. A horizontal depiction, in timeline style, of simultaneous historical, political, and cultural events.

Horowitz, Maryanne Cline. *The New Dictionary of the History of Ideas*. New York: Charles Scribner's Sons, 2004.

Jones, Judy, and William Wilson. *An Incomplete Education*. New York: Ballantine, 1995. Provides a variety of information not easily found, such as explanations for the job titles in film production credits.

Kane, Joseph Nathan, Steven Anzouin, and Janet Podell. *Famous First Facts: A Record of First Happenings, Discoveries, and Inventions in American History.* New York: Wilson, 1997.

Lapham, Lewis, Michael Pollan, and Eric Etheridge. *Harper's Index Book.* New York: Holt, 1987. Provides statistics with social and political implications— such as the number of millionaires on different presidents' cabinets, with references. See also individual issues of Harper's magazine since 1986, and the current month at http://www.harpers.org/

Mills, Jerry Leath, and Louis D. Rubin, eds. *A Writer's Companion: A Handy Compendium of Useful but Hard-to-Find Information on History, Literature, Art, Science, Travel, Philosophy, and Much More.* New York: HarperCollins, 1997.

Panati, Charles. *Extraordinary Origins of Everyday Things.* New York: HarperCollins, 1989. Inventions of common objects.

Wallechinsky, David, and Amy Wallace. *The Book of Lists.* New York: Warner, 1995. (See other books of lists in this series.)

RESOURCES FOR EVALUATING INFORMATION

about.com "urban legends"	http://urbanlegends.about.com/
email—reality checks	http://www.truthorfiction.com/
Evaluating chain letters	http://www.purportal.com/
Evaluating websites: criteria and tools	http://www.library.cornell.edu/olinuris/ref/research/webeval.html
Evaluation of information sources—includes links to informative articles	http://www.vuw.ac.nz/staff/alastair_smith/evaln/evaln.htm
FAIR (fairness and accuracy in reporting)	http://www.fair.org/

FactCheck (Annenberg School of Journalism at Univ. of Penn.)	http://www.factcheck. org/
List of Internet hoaxes	http://hoaxbusters.org/
Rob Rosenberger's virus myths	http://www.vmyths.com/
Symantec hoax page	http://www.symantec.com/ avcenter/hoax.html
Symantec virus list	http://www.sarc.com/avcenter/ vinfodb.html
Urban Legends	http://www.snopes.com/
Virtual Chase	http://www.virtualchase.com/ quality/

INDEX

ABOUT THE AUTHORS

As Chair of the English Department of Nassau Community College, **Diana Roberts Wienbroer** coordinated a department of 150 faculty members and served on the National Executive Council of the Association of Departments of English. Besides teaching writing for over thirty years, both in Texas and New York, she has studied and taught film criticism. She is also the author of *Rules of Thumb for Online Research*. Since her retirement from NCC, she has taught seminars on Internet research and effective business writing.

Elaine Hughes taught writing for more than twenty-five years, primarily at Hinds Community College in Raymond, Mississippi, and at Nassau Community College. After her retirement from NCC and her return to Mississippi, she conducted many writing workshops for the Esalen Institute and for other organizations. In 2000 she won a Mississippi Arts Council grant for creative nonfiction. She is also the author of *Writing from the Inner Self*. In 2001 Elaine Hughes passed away after more than twenty years of victories over breast cancer.

A graduate of Amherst College and the University of Virginia, **Jay Silverman** has received fellowships from the Fulbright-Hayes Foundation, the Andrew Mellon Foundation, and the National Endowment for the Humanities. Dr. Silverman has taught at Virginia Highlands Community College and at Nassau Community College where he received the Honors Program award for Excellence in Teaching and where he also teaches in the College Bound Program of the Nassau County Mental Health Association.

The authors have also written *Rules of Thumb: A Guide for Writers*, 6th Edition, *Rules of Thumb for Research*, *Shortcuts for the Student Writer*, and *Good Measures: A Practice Book to Accompany Rules of Thumb*, all available from McGraw-Hill.

CPSIA information can be obtained
at www.ICGtesting.com
Printed in the USA
FFOW03n2329190715
15258FF